EMBROIDERING
WITH
SILK RIBBON

To Massimo and Alessandro

A warm thanks to my dear friends who have helped me in carrying out some
of the works in this manual: Afre and Caterina Magrotti, Annamaria Crema,
Anna Vigo, Cinzia Canevari, Isabella Nidasio.

I would also like to thank Wanda di Lolo (Le Temps Passé in Alessandria)
who kindly allowed me to reproduce the pelmet depicted on pages 8 and 9.

Thanks also to Cristina Sperandeo who gave me the opportunity of writing this manual
and to Alberto Bertoldi, Meli Verga and Enrica Sacchi who supervised the work.

Editor: Cristina Sperandeo
Photography: Alberto Bertoldi
Graphic design and layout: Paola Masera and Amelia Verga
Translation: Chiara Tarsia

Library of Congress Cataloging-in-Publication Data Available
10 9 8 7 6 5 4 3 2 1

Published by Sterling Publishing Company, Inc.
387 Park Avenue South, New York, N.Y. 10016
First published in Italy by R.C.S. Libri S.p.A.
under the title *Ricamare con il Silk Ribbon*
© 1999 by R.C.S. Libri S.p.A., Milano
English translation © 2000 by Sterling Publishing
Distributed in Canada by Sterling Publishing
c/o Canadian Manda Group, One Atlantic Avenue, Suite 105
Toronto, Ontario, Canada M6K 3E7
Distributed in Great Britain and Europe by Cassell PLC
Wellington House, 125 Strand, London WC2R 0BB, England
Distributed in Australia by Capricorn Link (Australia) Pty Ltd.
P.O. Box 6651, Baulkham Hills, Business Centre, NSW 2153, Australia

Sterling ISBN 0-8069-5875-8

Donatella Ciotti

EMBROIDERING
WITH
SILK RIBBON

Sterling Publishing Co., Inc.
New York

CONTENTS

INTRODUCTION

Silk ribbons, generally used as decorations, are a recurring element in everyday life, and are often associated with special moments. A beautiful ribbon refines and enriches a gift, embellishes a bunch of flowers, enlivens a hairdo, and adorns hats, bags, and clothing.
Who has not admired the beautiful formal dresses, always rich in laces and ribbons, used on important occasions from baptisms to weddings?
Matching ribbons can give a different tone to our table on feast days and can be used as decorations to hang round the house or on the Christmas tree.

A ribbon often assumes symbolic values. We all know what a pink or light-blue ribbon hanging from a door means! Lovers of western films will no doubt remember the film She Wore a Yellow Ribbon (1949) by John Ford in which the main character sports a yellow ribbon to make a "beau" understand that she is in love with him. Americans welcome home their beloved with a yellow ribbon tied around trees; this

happened for the veterans of the Persian Gulf War and the hostages freed in Iran.

This manual offers a new way of using ribbons: embroidering with silk ribbons, an age-old English tradition. The ribbon used is very narrow and is suitable for all types of fabric because its softness allows it to be threaded through even the most closely-knit weft. It also regains its filminess once out of the fabric. This manual sets out step-by-step explanations of the various stitches which will enable you to make astonishingly beautiful projects, thanks also to the three-dimensional effect unique to this embroidering technique. You will thus be able to embellish a dress, decorate the rim of a hat, adorn an everyday bag or enrich an evening one.
You will easily be able to make doll lavender bags, jewel caskets and a host of other refined objects, from table cloths for celebrating important festivities to knick-knacks with which to decorate your home.

Donatella Ciotti

A BRIEF THE HISTORY OF SILK RIBBON

RIBBONS AND THE ORIGINS OF EMBROIDERY WITH SILK RIBBONS

Ribbons have always played an important and significant role in all civilizations, whether they were used as strings for practical and functional purposes, or as decorative ornaments.

In Ancient Greece, ribbons were woven in women's hair to enhance their hair arrangements.

In Rome, ribbons, refined with gold and jewels, were skillfully arranged in women's hair. Ribbons were also used to adorn clothes and to reveal, according to their decorations and colors, the social class of the person wearing them.

In Medieval Italy, ribbons were used to decorate the backs of chairs, to adorn canopies or to tie the heavy curtains which, during the winter months, helped protect against the cold. But it wasn't until silk reached Lyon in the 15th century that the widespread use of ribbons increased considerably. The Mediterranean climate, suitable for mulberries, the only food eaten by silkworms, fostered the production of the precious thread. When the Papal Court moved to Avignon, under the control of the King of France, and the city became an important center, demand for silk ribbons soared. Popes and their court proudly sported sumptuous clothes, decorated with gold edged ribbons or brocade ribbons which highlighted the rank of those wearing them.

In 1446, Louis XI for the first time invited Italian weavers to court so that they could teach their craft to the people of Lyon. The project was never happened, but various-sized looms were nonetheless made for working both silk and ribbons. Demand increased to such an extent that in 1560 in Lyon, which continued to be the center of silk production, over five thousand weavers were weaving ribbons, even costly and extravagant ones, while approximately forty-five miles further south the regions of Velzy and Saint-Etienne also held primacy in ribbons. In 1660, Saint-Etienne and its surrounding provinces boasted about eight thousand looms for ribbons and three hundred and seventy for braids. Demand intensified in the 17th century, considered by many to be the period of greatest diffusion of rich and elegant ribbons. Louis XIV even adorned his shoes with ribbons interwoven with jewels and, influenced by Italian fashion, he invited his Court to dress in an original and creative manner. Mademoiselle de Fontagnes, for example, made her name in history when, during a formal hunting shoot, she used her ribbon garter to tie her tousled hair in order to make herself more presentable to the King. She thus launched a new fashion, still known today as chignon or

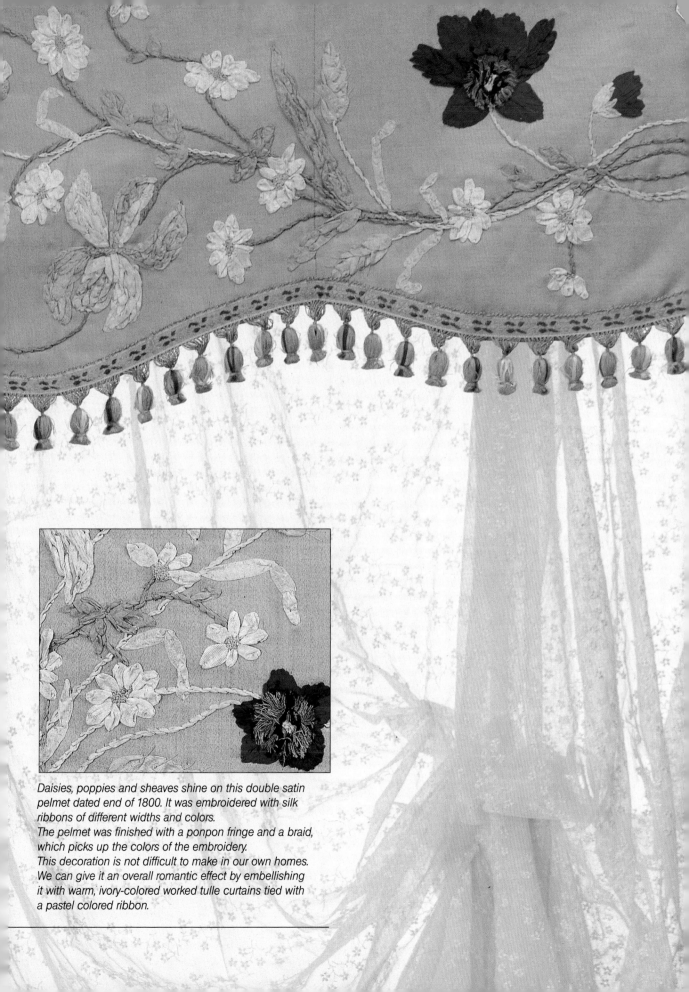

Daisies, poppies and sheaves shine on this double satin
pelmet dated end of 1800. It was embroidered with silk
ribbons of different widths and colors.
The pelmet was finished with a ponpon fringe and a braid,
which picks up the colors of the embroidery.
This decoration is not difficult to make in our own homes.
We can give it an overall romantic effect by embellishing
it with warm, ivory-colored worked tulle curtains tied with
a pastel colored ribbon.

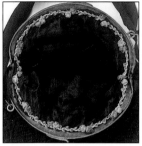

French knot. During the frevolously styled Rococo period, Louis XV loved embroidering and wrapping up little objects to give to the court ladies. Round about this time, clothes became more loose-fitting and flowing, and were replete with ribbons. The "Frill dress", characterized by pleats loosened on the chest and numerous ribbons, became extremely popular. It had been tailored especially for Madame de Montespan, one of Louis XVI's court ladies, who wanted to hide the fact that she was pregnant and thus prevent scandal-mongers from gossiping about her.

It was in this Rococo period in France that embroidery with silk ribbons began to appear. For decades ladies embroidered their dresses with silk ribbons. Their bodices were enriched with small roses rococo-style, with leaves and a myriad of scattered flowers, and were enriched with pearl beads and crystals. Women's lingerie became increasingly more sumptuous and refined, an integral part of their clothing apparel. Artisan laboratories rapidly started to crop up bearing the title "Suppliers to the Royal Household" where, with needles and ribbons, masterpieces were made which can still be admired today in the Museums of London and Pretoria, South Africa. From France, this type of embroidery soon passed on to other European countries, especially to England and from here to its colonies overseas, to America, New Zealand and Australia. The period in which this art (as embroidery was considered by American and Australian women) flourished at its utmost was between 1870 and 1880, when it became fashionable to embroider, besides dresses, also parasols, lampshades, "Crazy Quilts", knick-knacks for the home

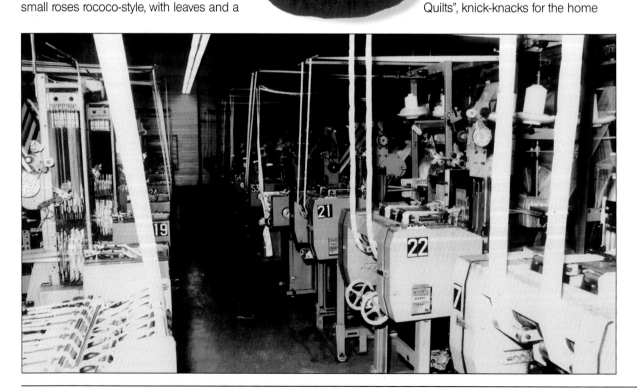

and millinery items. After the Second World War, female forms of art began to lose importance, but from 1980 to date there has been a certain revival. Embroidery has reawakened great interest and has regained its old splendor. Ribbon embroidery in particular is fun, easy and quick to do as it utilizes some simple, well-known traditional embroidery techniques. It is highly regarded and admired especially for its characteristic three-dimensional effect, given by the ribbons used, always soft, ductile and filmy.

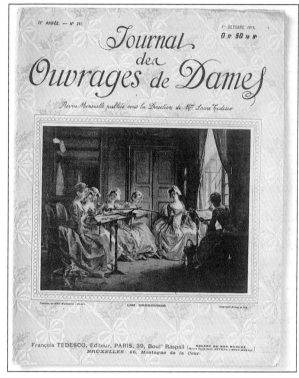

On the opposite page:
A handmade silk evening bag embroidered in the Florentine style; a border of small rococo-style roses made with soft pastel-colored silk ribbons was embroidered on the inside to hide the seams. A black silk ribbon was fastened to the zip of the bag, transforming it into a shoulder bag.

A series of looms, which still operate today, make ribbons by the meter.

On this page:
The frontispiece of a 1911 French magazine and two pictures representing rococo-style embroideries, at that time much in fashion.

TECHNIQUE

Anemone

Anthurium

Aster

Gypsophilia

Begonia

Begonia

Strelitzia

Dicentra

Bluebell

Buttercup

Pot marigold

Calla

Camellia

Carnation

Chrysanthemum

Clematis

Columbine

Rudbeckia

Fleur-de-lis

Cosmos

Crocus

Cyclamen

Narcissus

Daffodil

Dahlia

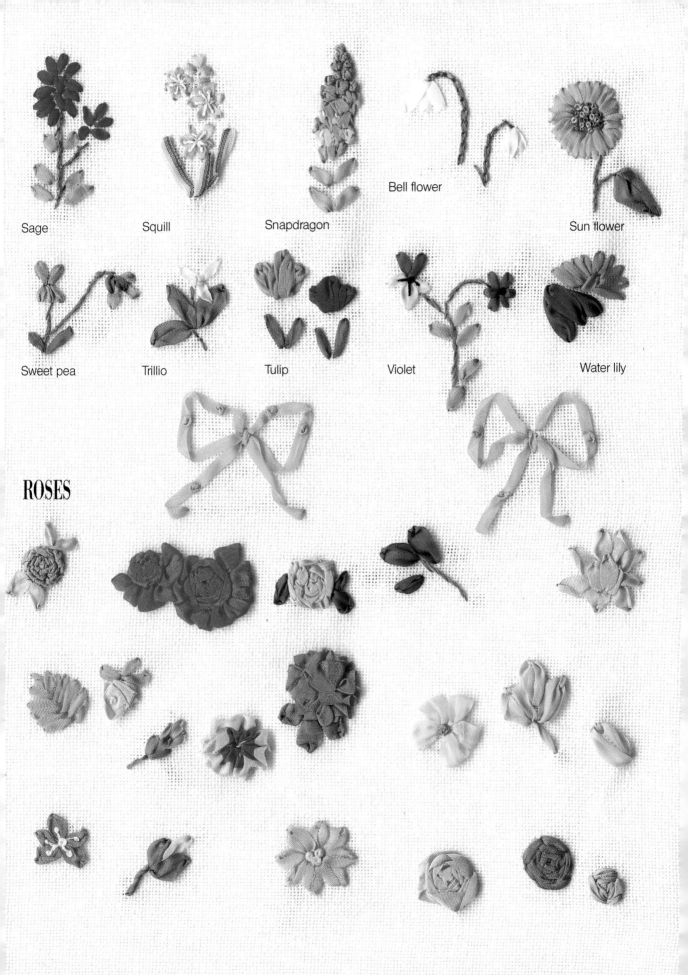

Sage

Squill

Snapdragon

Bell flower

Sun flower

Sweet pea

Trillio

Tulip

Violet

Water lily

ROSES

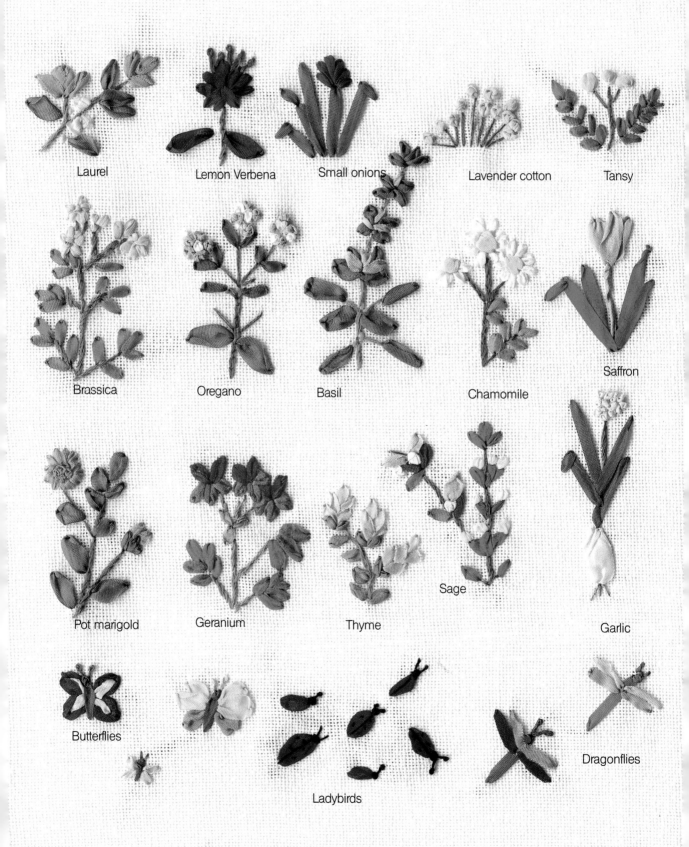

Laurel

Lemon Verbena

Small onions

Lavender cotton

Tansy

Brassica

Oregano

Basil

Chamomile

Saffron

Pot marigold

Geranium

Thyme

Sage

Garlic

Butterflies

Ladybirds

Dragonflies

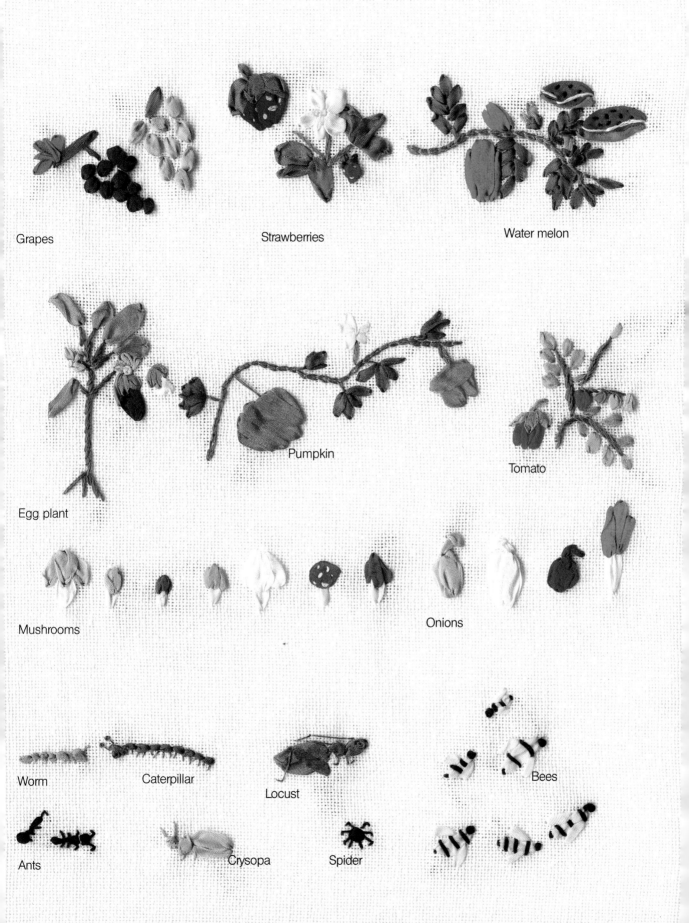

Grapes

Strawberries

Water melon

Egg plant

Pumpkin

Tomato

Mushrooms

Onions

Worm

Caterpillar

Locust

Bees

Ants

Crysopa

Spider

NEEDLES

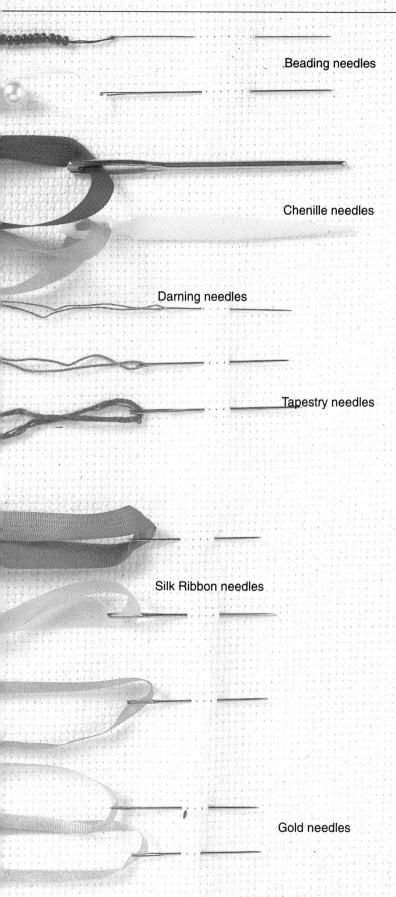

Beading needles

Chenille needles

Darning needles

Tapestry needles

Silk Ribbon needles

Gold needles

In the beginning people used pierced thorns or fish bones as needles to join skins or pieces of fabric. Since then, the needle has undergone a huge transformation. Today needles of various types, sizes and caliber are available on the market.

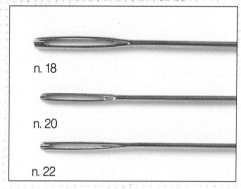

n. 18

n. 20

n. 22

Various kinds of needles are used in embroidery: fine needles for light fabrics and large needles for thick materials.
In silk ribbon embroidery, needles must be particularly sharp, so that they can be drawn smoothly through the fabric without creating unattractive pulled threads, and they must have a long eye for the thread to pass easily through and for it to slide freely without twisting. For ribbons from 9/32–12/32–15/32" (7–9–12 mm), use needles ranging from n° 18 to n° 22, while n° 24 is suitable for 3/32" (3 mm) ribbons.

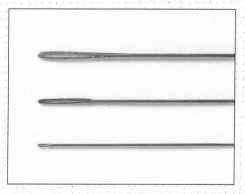

The gold needle (see some examples above) has a special galvanic covering which protects it from contact with particular acid perspiration which first oxidizes and then rusts all metals, and prevents in the specific case the normal run of the needle in the fabric warp.

RIBBONS

There are an incredible variety of ribbons available on the market today. They can be divided into two basic categories: washable ribbons and ornamental ribbons. *Washable ribbons* are made of narrow fabric with high quality selvages to meet the needs of the clothing and furnishing industry. They come with detailed instructions regarding washing, preserving colors and ironing.

Decorative or ornamental ribbons are used exclusively for decorating. Many of these have no edge, but are stiffened through particular processes so that they do not fray during use. There are also ribbons with a fine metallic backing incorporated in the selvages, which gives them shape. These are used to embellish packages or decorate the table. These ribbons are not washable, therefore before beginning a piece of embroidery with ribbons, be sure to check these particulars.

Silk ribbons – These are available in various sizes from 3/32–9/32–12/32–15/32" (3–7–9–12 mm) and in various colors. They can be used for embroidery on any type of fabric. They can be washed in water with soap, whether liquid or flakes, and are ironed on the back so as not to flatten them. Certain colors, such as magenta and burgundy, must be dampened before use to avoid that while drying, unattractive marks are formed, which could damage the embroidery.

Organdie ribbons – They are used where the embroidery needs volume and transparency. They come in various widths.

Embroidery threads – These are used to create the weft of certain stitches or to fasten the ribbons on the back at the end of the work.

Beads and glass beads – These come in various shapes and are usually used to embellish and give luminosity to the embroidery.

DECORATING RIBBONS

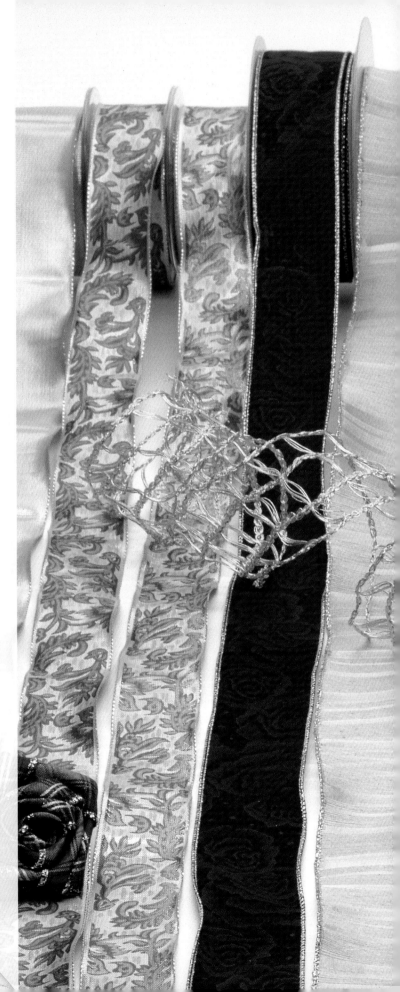

These ribbons are sold by the meter or already cut into determined lengths. Ribbons for decoration are of various types.

Voile ribbons - Printed smooth or with a strip of satin incorporated, they are used to make small manually worked roses, which are then sewed on to decorate hats and bags, or used to give finishing touches when wrapping gift packages, or again as place markers on the festive table for important occasions.

Satin ribbons − They can be smooth, rucked or pleated. Wefts of considerable flexibility can be obtained through their use.

Lace ribbons − Embellished with pearls or rucked, they are used in embroidery, or as decorations for special occasions.

The projects set out are easy to make and designed for present day life styles. Change the color shadings as you please; the results will be just as attractive. There is no fixed rule for matching colors. Sometimes contrasting colors put side by side can create a very stimulating effect. The shade-on-shade colors are very sophisticated and if you choose pastel hues, the effect will be that of old family souvenirs. Pastel colors are very romantic and feminine, and the intermediate shades very relaxing and attractive to the eye.

By observing nature, that inexhaustible source of color and inspiration, you will become more experienced with every day that passes and be on the constant lookout for every new and eye-catching color schemes.

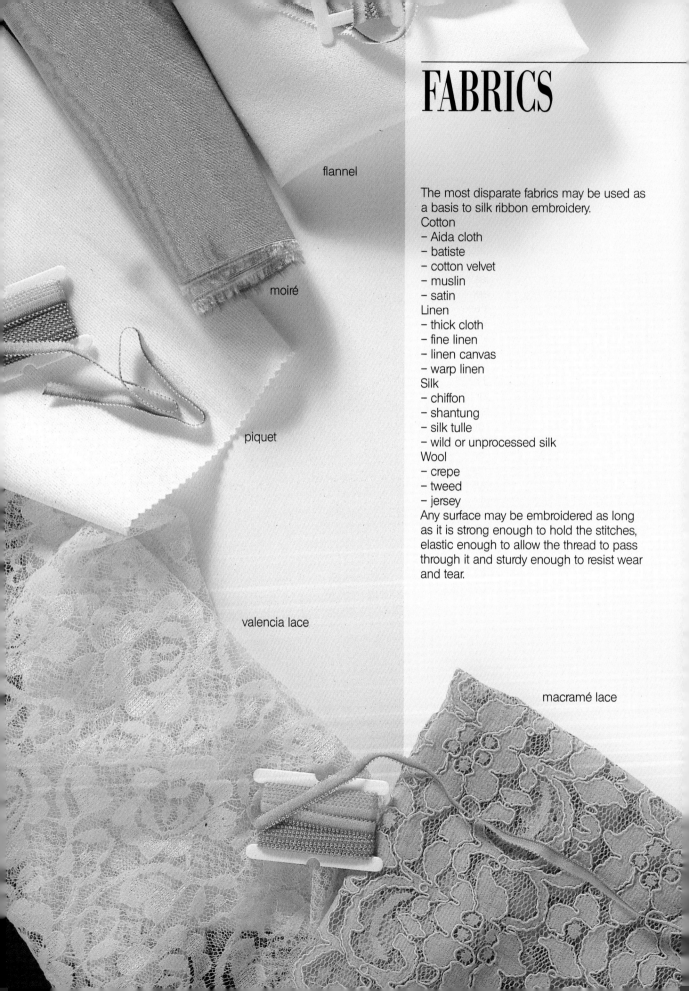

FABRICS

flannel

moiré

piquet

valencia lace

macramé lace

The most disparate fabrics may be used as a basis to silk ribbon embroidery.

Cotton
– Aida cloth
– batiste
– cotton velvet
– muslin
– satin

Linen
– thick cloth
– fine linen
– linen canvas
– warp linen

Silk
– chiffon
– shantung
– silk tulle
– wild or unprocessed silk

Wool
– crepe
– tweed
– jersey

Any surface may be embroidered as long as it is strong enough to hold the stitches, elastic enough to allow the thread to pass through it and sturdy enough to resist wear and tear.

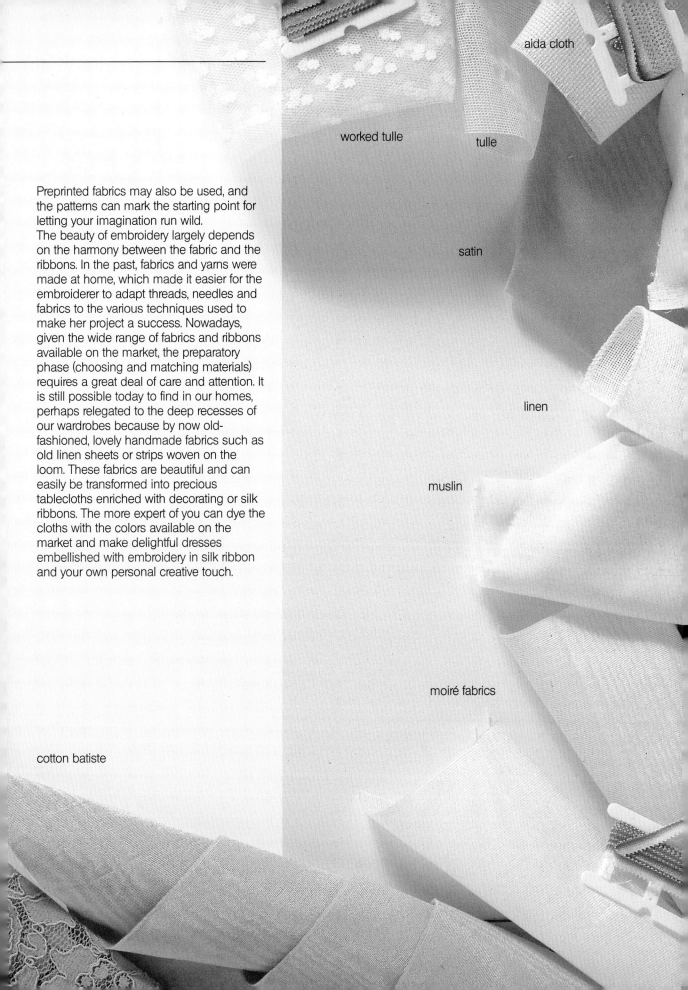

aida cloth

worked tulle

tulle

satin

linen

muslin

moiré fabrics

Preprinted fabrics may also be used, and the patterns can mark the starting point for letting your imagination run wild.

The beauty of embroidery largely depends on the harmony between the fabric and the ribbons. In the past, fabrics and yarns were made at home, which made it easier for the embroiderer to adapt threads, needles and fabrics to the various techniques used to make her project a success. Nowadays, given the wide range of fabrics and ribbons available on the market, the preparatory phase (choosing and matching materials) requires a great deal of care and attention. It is still possible today to find in our homes, perhaps relegated to the deep recesses of our wardrobes because by now old-fashioned, lovely handmade fabrics such as old linen sheets or strips woven on the loom. These fabrics are beautiful and can easily be transformed into precious tablecloths enriched with decorating or silk ribbons. The more expert of you can dye the cloths with the colors available on the market and make delightful dresses embellished with embroidery in silk ribbon and your own personal creative touch.

cotton batiste

MOUNTING MATERIAL ON THE FRAME

The rings making up the frames serve to keep the material taut during working and to guarantee a smooth end result. Even to those of you who tend to pull the stitch too hard can keep the ribbon a little slacker, and this gives the embroidery more volume and a three-dimensional effect.

The ring frame, known also as the drum frame, is available in a variety of sizes and consists of two simple rings, one fitting inside the other, kept tightly together by an adjustable screw on the outer ring. This type of frame is used for small embroideries and is easily mounted.

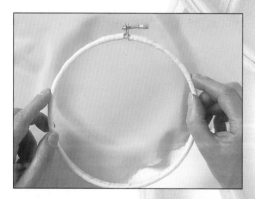

Place the material over the smaller ring and then place the outer ring over the material. Tighten the screw until the fabric is held quite taut. Having tightened the outer ring, do not pull the fabric anymore to avoid damaging it.

BINDING A FRAME

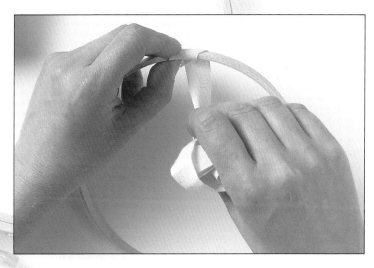

To bind a ring frame, cover one of the two rings with soft tape. Pull to avoid forming folds. Fasten the ends of the tape with small stitches. Do the same with the other ring. If you do not have any tape handy, you may use strips of fine gauze.

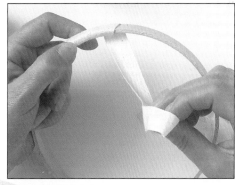

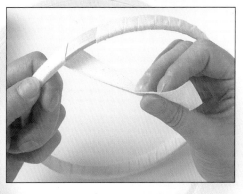

Binding the ring frame is an extremely useful operation as it helps to prevent fine fabrics such as silk, organdie or velvet from being spoilt by unattractive marks, dents or flattening of the pile which is then difficult to raise again.

PREPRINTED PATTERNS

Preprinted kits complete with material and instructions are available on the market. Embroidery lovers can get inspiration from these kits and if they like, and can embroider the proposed pattern and embellish it with details worked with silk ribbon.

It is advisable to work with ribbons, which are not longer than 20" (50 cm) in order to prevent them from getting twisted. Should this happen, just let the needle fall perpendicularly and the ribbon will free itself automatically. By combining ribbons with traditional embroidery threads, original results can be achieved.

TRANSFERRING DESIGNS

Before starting to embroider, you must first decide on the type of pattern you would like to design, as well as the fabric and ribbon to use.

As you plan your design, decide how to transfer the pattern onto the material, unless you'd rather try your hand with preprinted patterns. There are different ways of designing a pattern onto fabric:

PREPRINTED

These are patterns drawn by a designer. They are preprinted and are normally used for tablecloths and cushions.

TRACEABLE PATTERNS

They are printed on copy paper with special inks and are transferred by placing the side with the ink on to the fabric.

TRACING PENCIL

This is used to transfer a pre-drawn pattern. Place a sheet of copy paper on the pattern, go over it with a tracing pencil and then transfer the pattern onto the fabric you are planning to embroider, ironing it without steam. It is advisable to use the right temperature for the type of fabric you are using, as temperatures which are too high tend to yellow cloth. If, during the transfer phase, mistakes are made, it is possible to wash the item in warm, soapy water. The design traced on tissue paper can only be used once; for a larger or continual design the initial pattern must be traced again.

Designs transferred with tracing pencil

TRACING WITH CARBON PAPER

This technique is suitable for materials with smooth surfaces. Place the carbon paper – dark for light-colored fabrics, light for dark-colored ones – between the material and the tracing. Use a pencil to outline the design, taking care not to press too hard the parts that are not to be traced to avoid unattractive smudges appearing on the fabric.

DIRECT TRACING

This method is suitable for very fine materials, such as organdie, muslin, batiste and voile, because their transparency makes it possible to trace the design directly.

TRACING WITH RICE PAPER

This paper is not only used for normal tracing operations, but also as an embroidery cloth for special fabrics, where tracing with the iron or other techniques could compromise the end result. Proceed as follows: after drawing your design on the rice paper, crumple it slightly without tearing it, tack in on to the fabric and then proceed as you would for normal embroidery. When you have finished, tear away the paper. You will now find the embroidery fastened to the fabric.
You can fill in the empty parts by embellishing the embroidery with bead or flower compositions, or whatever else takes your fancy.

Preprinted designs in indelible ink

LOOP STITCH

STRAIGHT STITCH

BULLION STITCH

MONTANO KNOT

LAZY DAISY

RIBBON STITCH

MONTANO KNOT

FEATHER STITCH

LOOP STITCH

FLY STITCH

STRAIGHT STITCH

SPIDER WEB ROSE

MONTANO KNOT

BULLION STITCH

PRICKING AND POUNCING

Place the tracing paper on the pattern to be traced and, using a ballpoint pen, carefully draw round the entire outline.

Remove the traced design. With a pin, prick closely along the lines of the design, making sure not to overlook the more difficult parts.

Place the pricked pattern on the fabric, holding it in place with some pins, then rub pounce powder over it.

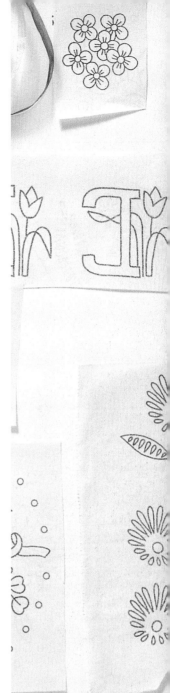

This is a traditional technique which gives excellent results and is suitable for all types of smooth fabrics. For this process you will need:
- *pounce powder*
- *pin or needle for pricking the paper*
- *drawing pins*
- *a soft pad*

Dip the soft pad into the pounce powder and rub it all over the pricked holes, tapping slightly so that the powder penetrates right through the holes to the fabric.

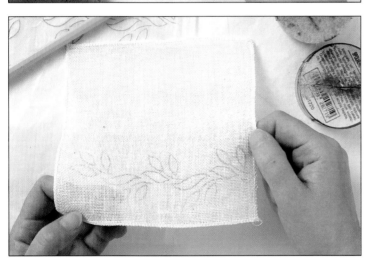

Carefully remove the paper to avoid smudging. Should the drawing appear incomplete, draw the missing parts with a soft pencil. If you do not intend to carry on with the work immediately, it is advisable to iron the drawing without steam for it to last longer.

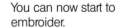

You can now start to embroider.

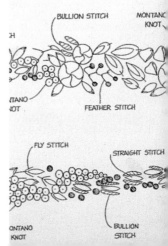

BULLION STITCH   MONTANO KNOT

FEATHER STITCH

FLY STITCH   STRAIGHT STITCH

MONTANO KNOT   BULLION STITCH

STITCHES

TO START

To begin, procure a ribbon about 20" (50 cm) long. Thread it through the eye of the needle, fold it a couple of inches back on itself and pass the tip of the needle through the center.

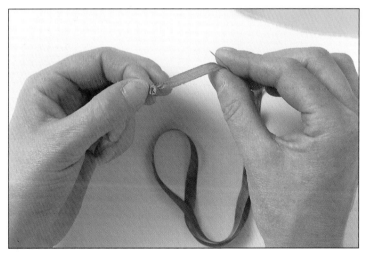

Make a knot by holding the ribbon in one hand and pulling it with the other.

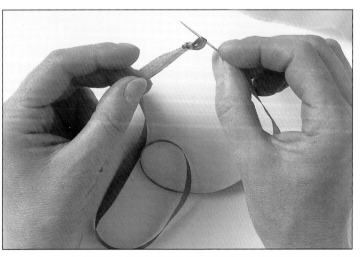

A knot made in this way is considered a flat knot, which, unlike the traditional one, has no thickness.

Unlike traditional embroidery, where the starting thread is worked without knots to avoid unattractive shiny spots during ironing, in silk ribbon embroidery a flat knot is used, giving the ribbon a solid support and preventing it from slipping out of the fabric during the various steps.

FASTENING A STITCH

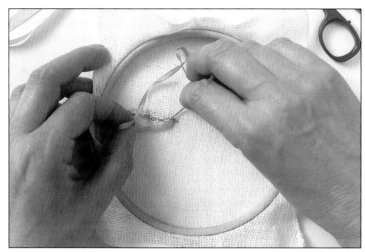

After having finished the work, fasten off the ribbon by threading it through to the wrong side of the fabric and pass the needle very carefully under the embroidered stitches, forming a little loop.

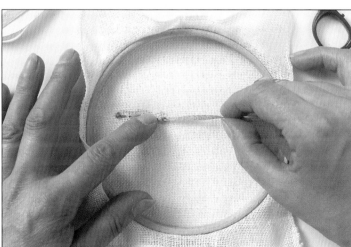

Use your fingers to hold down the stitches, so that they do not appear on the back, and then pull the ribbon slightly.

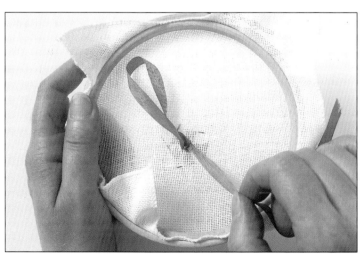

Once you've finished the work, cut the ribbon a couple of inches away from the last stitch.

In some cases it is advisable to fasten off the ribbon directly to the fabric with small stitches using mouliné thread.

CHAIN STITCH

This stitch is often used to border napkins or to cover seams in "crazy patchwork",

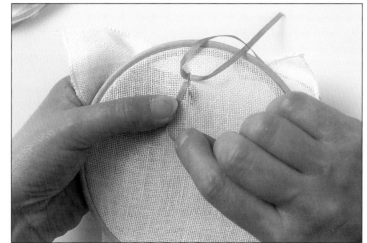

Pass the ribbon from the wrong side of the fabric to the front. Insert the needle into roughly the same point from which it came out and take it out again a short distance below. Hook the ring thus formed and pull the ribbon.

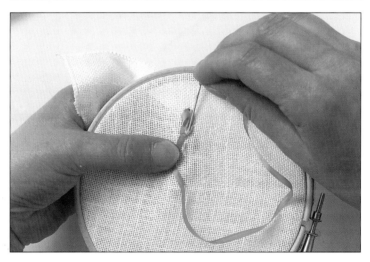

Return with the tip of the needle into the newly created ring and make a new one identical to the previous one.

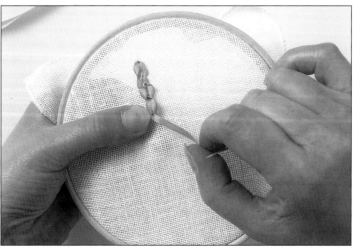

Proceed in this way until you have embroidered a small chain.

FLY STITCH

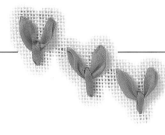

This is a minute stitch, suitable for borders and ideal for finishing baby clothes. It can be worked both horizontally and vertically. Embroidered with ribbons, it gives the effect of many butterflies.

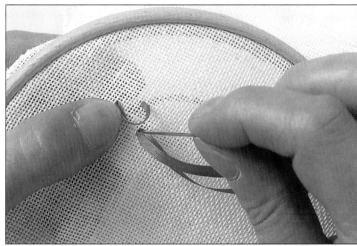

Pull the ribbon through to the front on the top left. Slant it downwards and, holding it firmly in place with the thumb of your hand, bring the needle to the top right, at the same height from which it came out.

Bring the needle out at the center of the stitch made.

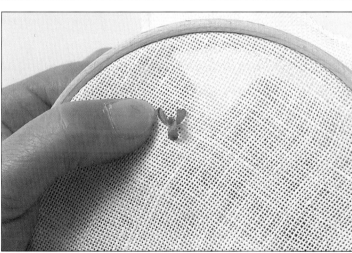

Fasten the stitch through a small stitch bridging the previous one and at the same time bring the needle up at the top right to make the next stitch.

KNOTTED STITCHES ⊙

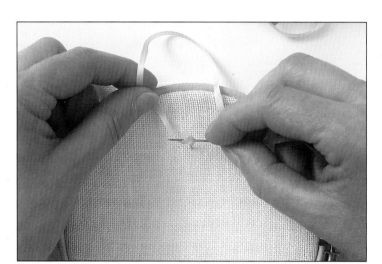

Bring the needle out to the front of the work and hold it down with the other hand. Wrap the ribbon twice around the needle. Continuing to keep the ribbon down, make sure the twistings do not overlap. Then re-insert the needle to the back of the fabric, if possible at the same point from which it came out.

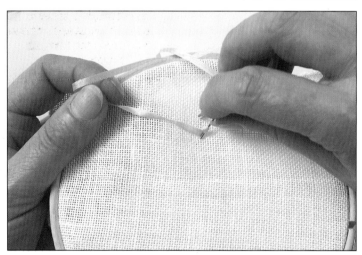

Follow the ribbon with your fingertips to avoid knots being formed when pulling it through.

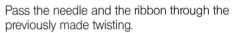

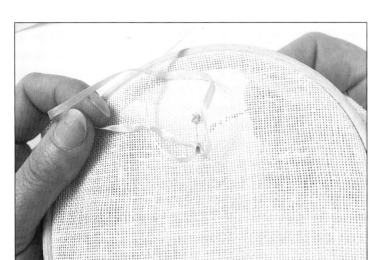

Pass the needle and the ribbon through the previously made twisting.

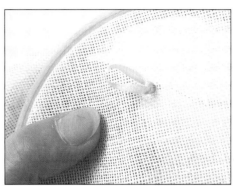

When working with ribbons, it is easier to make and finish off each single knot instead of running the needle along the back, as this prevents using too much ribbon.

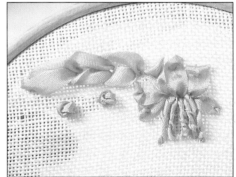

This is a filling up stitch, which is often used to make flowers.

COUCHING

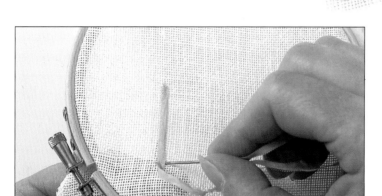

This may be used as an outline stitch or to give a finishing touch to a letter. Two ribbons of different colors may also be used—one for the base and the other for the little bridges.

Bring the ribbon to the front of the work, and lay it to the required length. This can be done either horizontally or vertically.

Bring the ribbon once more to the back, keeping it flat on the fabric.

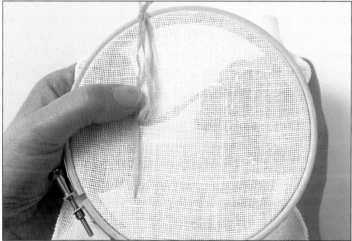

Return to the front of the work and fasten the ribbon with bridging stitches, at right angles, making sure to keep the distance between the bridge as regular as possible.

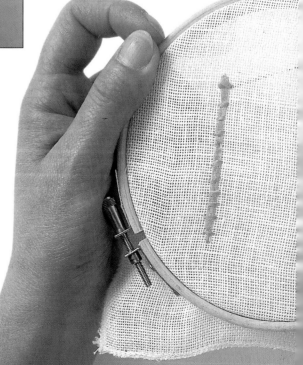

The bridging stitches in these photographs have been left slack on purpose to make them more evident.

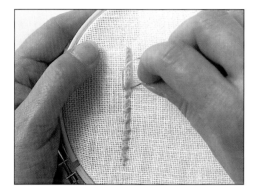

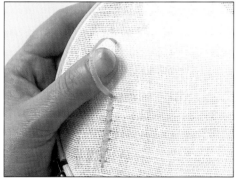

At the end of the work, bring the ribbon to the back and fasten it.

FERN STITCH

Bring the needle to the front of the work and make a vertical stitch (straight stitch) and then bring it to the back once more.

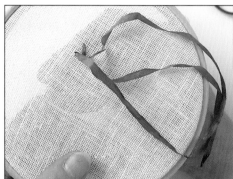

Bring the needle out at the top left and pass it back again at the bottom right. This is the beginning of the leaf.

Bring the needle out to the right, then back in at the center, lower down, exactly under the vertical stitch.

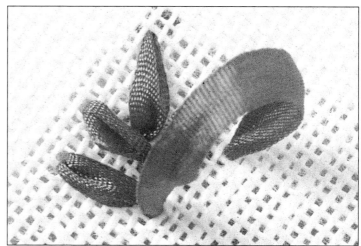

Continue with increasing stitches worked alternately on the right and on the left under the base of the previous stitches.

With a small vertical stitch, make the petiole of the leaf. Remember always to keep the ribbon slack.

By using two needles you can use two ribbons of different colors to create nuances.

FEATHER STITCH

The Feather Stitch is perfect for making flower cups.

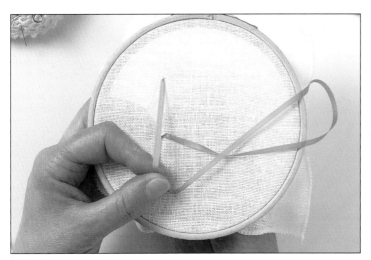

Bring the needle out to the front of the work, keeping the ribbon very flat and taut. With the help of your thumb, make a loop and return to the back, keeping the ribbon flat.

Return to the front of the work, passing from the base of the previous loop without pulling.

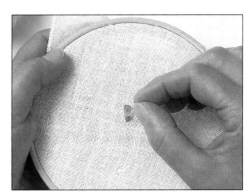

A chain of loops bound together is thus formed.

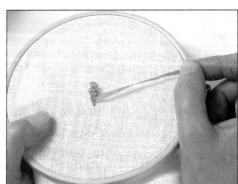

LOOP STITCH

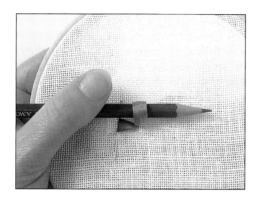

Bring out the needle to the front of the work, then insert it immediately behind the exit point and return to the back again, gently pulling the ribbon so as to form a loop. To give roundness to the loop, insert a pencil.

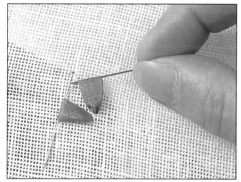

Bring the needle once more to the front and proceed as before. Once the first loop has been formed, fasten it with a pin at the width required so as to prevent the ribbon from slipping back or rucking.

Give the embroidery a circular shape and fasten always the loops with pins. When five or six petals have been made, fasten off the ribbon. Then fill in the center of the flower with some knotted stitches or small beads.

You may now remove the pins as your flower is finished. If you wish, add some small leaves to the embroidery.

To obtain three dimensional flowers, use ribbons of 9/32–12/32 " (7–9 mm).

RUNNING STITCH

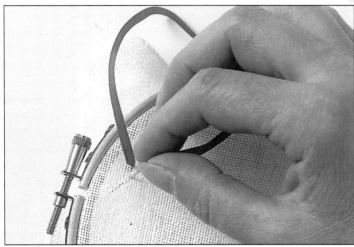

Bring the needle to the front of the work and fill in a small space of fabric with a knot.

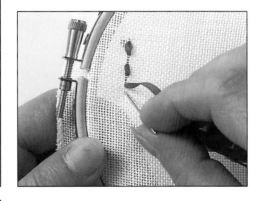

Insert the needle again, making sure to leave the same amount of fabric between one stitch and the other, and then repeat the first stitch.

When working with a ribbon, remember to keep it down with the index and thumb of your other hand to avoid it curling on itself and losing its softness.

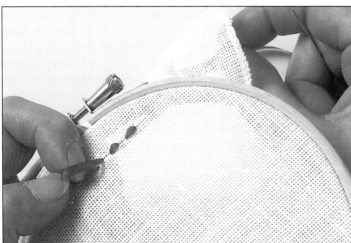

When you have covered the surface desired, go back and fill in the empty spaces.

This stitch is ideal for softening the outline of an object or for writing words or phrases. It is often found in cross stitch embroidery. It is generally used to give more depth to the embroidery, but may also be used as a basis for making flower stems.

LAZY DASY STITCH

This is one of the variations of chain stitch.

Bring the needle to the front of the work and then insert it a little further below, forming a loop around the tip of the needle.

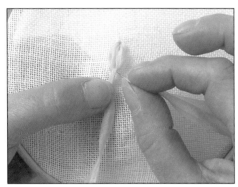

Pull the ribbon slightly, pass the needle through the loop once more and fasten it to the fabric with a small knot.

Bring the needle to the base of the stitch to form a petal. Proceed in this manner for the other petals (usually at least five). Lastly, fasten off the ribbon at the back.

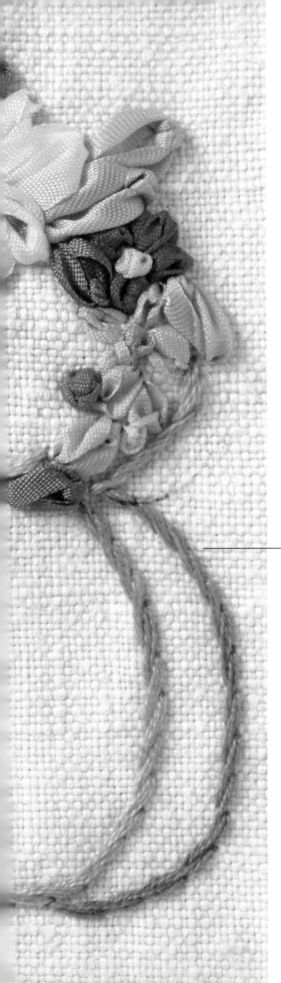

TWISTED CHAIN

Bring the needle to the front of the work and with a movement from the top towards the bottom, cross the fabric, keeping the needle slightly slanted and the ribbon flat. Then return to the back.

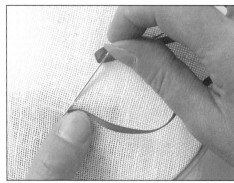

Bring the needle again to the front of the work in the middle of the previous stitch. Proceed, keeping the ribbon in the same slanting position. The flatter the ribbon, the more the linearity of the stitch is highlighted.

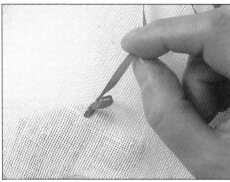

Note: In many cases, for example when filling small spaces, it is best to use mouliné thread.

This stitch is one of the main embroidery stitches and can be used to make the background of other stitches, outlines, curved or straight lines. To give the idea of more space, insert the needle into the fabric in a slightly slanted manner.

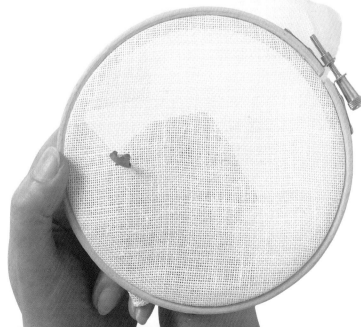

RIBBON STITCH

This is quite certainly the best known and most used stitch. It is employed to make petals, leaves and many other motifs.

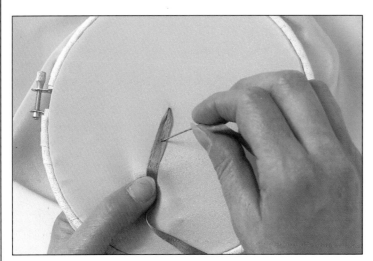

Bring out the needle on the front side and, with the help of your thumb, hold the ribbon flat on the fabric and bring it towards you. When you've reached the right length for the petal, insert the needle half way down through the ribbon and the fabric to the back of the work.

Pull the ribbon until a hole has been made, then proceed carefully to create the shape of a petal. If you pull too quickly, you will merely obtain a slender line of ribbon, which you cannot adjust.

To obtain a filmy stitch pull slowly until a small curl is formed on the top. Make the other petals in the same way.

Here is a small bag in white linen embroidered in ribbon stitch and knotted stitch.

TWISTED RIBBON STITCH

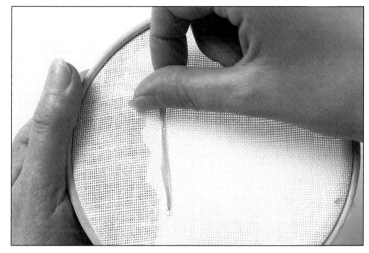

This stitch is normally used to make flower stems or abstract work as wished.

Bring the needle to the front of the fabric and twist the ribbon round itself for the length required.

Bring the ribbon to the back of the fabric. Repeat these steps, keeping the ribbon slack.

Examples of twisted ribbon stitch.

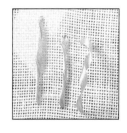

PISTIL STITCH

Bring out the needle on the front of the work and, with the help of your other hand, keep the ribbon taut on the fabric to prevent it from rolling around itself.

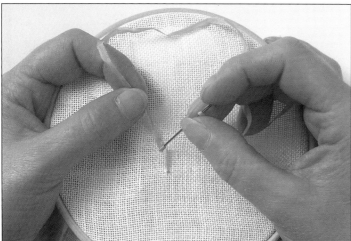

Wrap the ribbon around the needle as for the knotted stitch.

Insert the needle in the fabric, regulating the tension of the ribbon with your left hand so that no other knots, difficult to undo, should form during the operation. Then reinsert in the fabric from the back.

This stitch can be used not only to make flower pistils, but also to invent other motifs as you please for insertion as decoration in your embroidery.

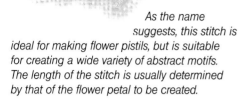

As the name suggests, this stitch is ideal for making flower pistils, but is suitable for creating a wide variety of abstract motifs. The length of the stitch is usually determined by that of the flower petal to be created.

In this embroidery on the right the fuchsia pistils have been created with double mouliné thread in order not to weigh down the gauzy corolla.

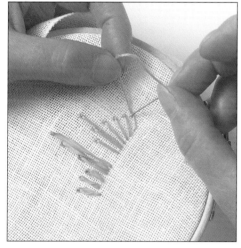

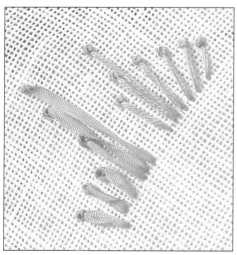

CORAL STITCH

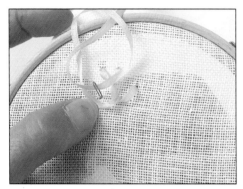

This is a filling up stitch, light and delicate, suitable for obtaining a feathery effect.

Bring the ribbon out on the top of the fabric to be worked and make a long, slack stitch.

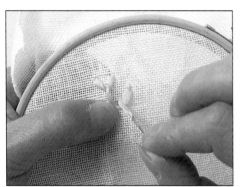

Pass the needle on the front through the fabric and over the ribbon with which you are working. Pull the ribbon.

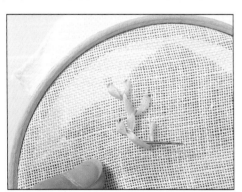

Continue in this way, alternating the stitches to the right and to the left.

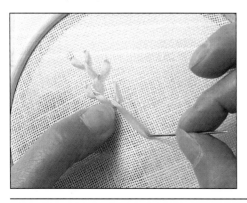

Reduce the length of the single stitches to create the shapes you desire.

CROSS STITCH

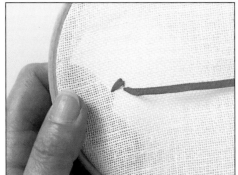

Make a starting knot and bring the needle and the ribbon to the front of the work and make a diagonal stitch keeping the ribbon flat on the fabric. Return to the back of the work.

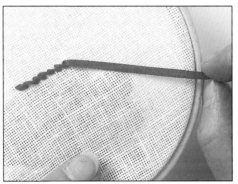

Return to the front and cover the stitch just made with a diagonal stitch.

This is one of the oldest stitches in embroidery. It has been used since man first learned to sew and was widely used in Phrygia. In ancient Egypt, it turns up in the traditional embroidery of many lands such as the Greek islands, Turkey, Austria. It is used for borders, outlines and to fill in where necessary.

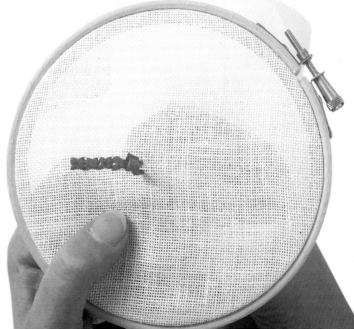

WEAVING STITCH

This is an easy stitch and it is suitable for filling in both motifs and backgrounds. The sheen of the silk ribbons is often a sufficient decoration motif, therefore the stitches can be of the simplest, and worked in the fabric itself.

Come out on the front of the work and make a series of flat stitches of the desired length. Having covered the required surface bring the needle to the back and fasten off.

With a different colored ribbon, come out on the front of the work and pass the needle under the flat stitches.

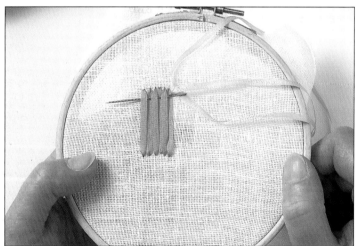

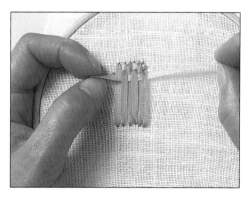

Alternate the passing of the ribbon now over, now under the series of flat stitches until all has been covered, then return to the back of the work.

Repeat these steps until the space involved has been covered. A grill anchored to the fabric has thus been made. This motif is

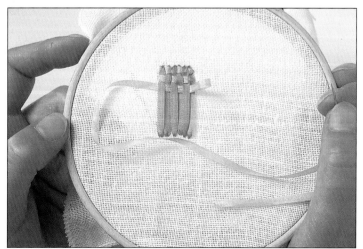

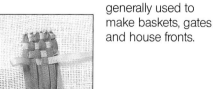

generally used to make baskets, gates and house fronts.

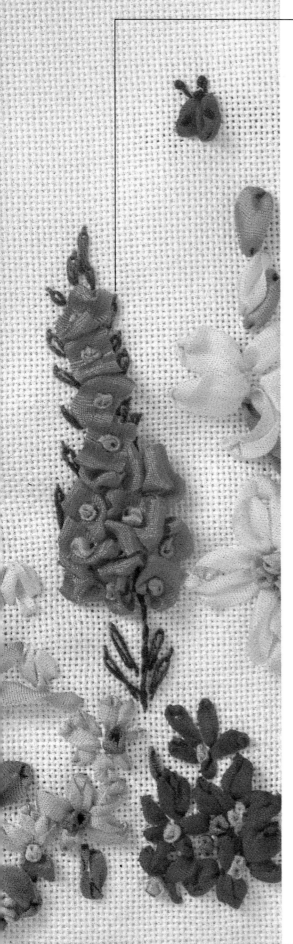

DECORATED LOOP STITCH

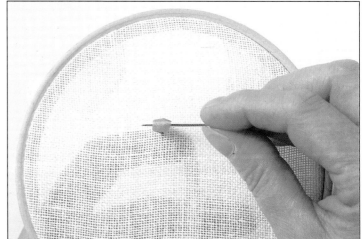

Bring the ribbon out to the front part of your work, keep it smooth with your index and thumb and draw it through to the back of the fabric.

Keep the loop formed wide open. Return to the front of the work and with the needle make many loops of the same size in the same manner.

This stitch is usually used as a filling stitch, but it can also be used to make flowers. If it is fastened tightly to the fabric, it is suitable for embroidering clothes, bed linen and napkins. It differs from the loophole in that the center of the loop is finished off with a knotted stitch or a bead.

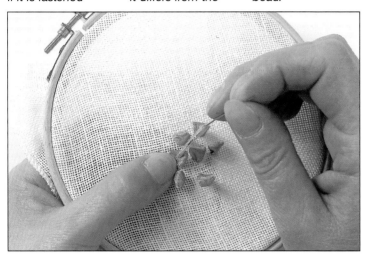

With a contrasting ribbon, enter the loop from the back and go out again at the center of the loop, then flatten it with your thumb. Now make a knotted stitch.

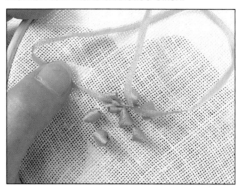

An example of loops embroidered with a knotted stitch at the center, worked in double or treble mouliné thread.

White linen bag embroidered using the decorated loop stitch technique and tied with a wide yellow ribbon.

ZIGZAG RUNNING STITCH

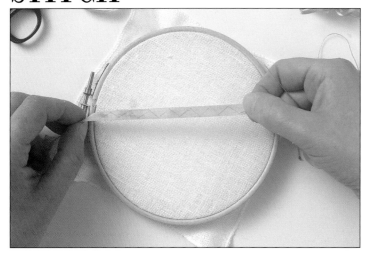

Using a pencil, draw a zigzag on the ribbon.

Follow the sketched lines and make a series of small running stitches using thread of the same colors.

Ruck slightly so as to form a sequence of petals.

Sew the petals in circles with small hidden stitches. Apply the motif to the fabric in the same manner.

Make a small-knotted stitch in the middle to obtain a flower with its pistil. Finish off with branches and leaves.

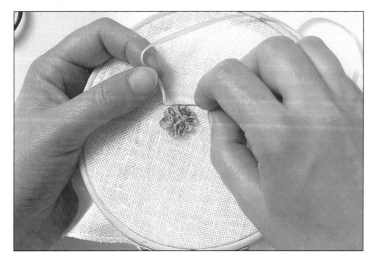

The running stitch is the main stitch in sewing. It is used in embroidery to make lines and outlines and as a background for other stitches. It is carried out in one go, passing the needle in and out of the fabric at regular intervals.

STRAIGHT STITCH

It is one of the oldest stitches in embroidery and sewing. Made up of different-sized linear stitches, it is universally used to make petals, leaves and friezes.

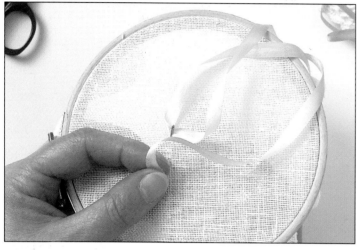

Bring the needle out to the front of your work.

With the other hand bring the ribbon to the back, keeping it close to the fabric so that it doesn't twist.

Repeat the stitch to suit your fancy, giving shape to your embroidery.

A combination of two stitches worked together to create a more accentuated effect both in relief and in decoration. Once the basic stitch is made, it is preferable to use a blunt needle, to avoid damaging the ribbon during winding.

BULLION STITCH

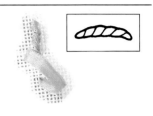

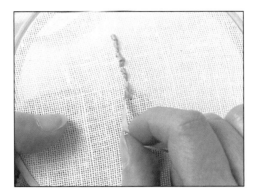

Make a series of bullion stitches of the length desired.

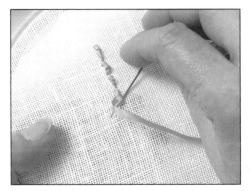

Then bring the needle out to the back of your work. Return to the front and with winding and oblique stitches fill the spaces, without touching the fabric.

Small padded stitches will thus be formed. Worked in circles, they give the idea of soft petals, reminiscent of the filmy stitch, so dear to our mothers.

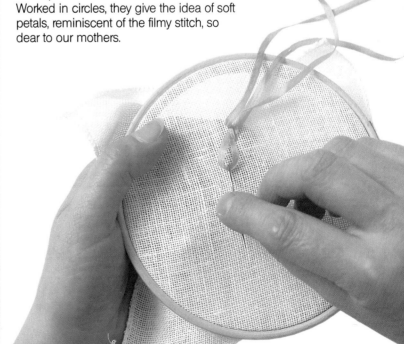

RUNNING STITCH RUCKED AT THE CENTER

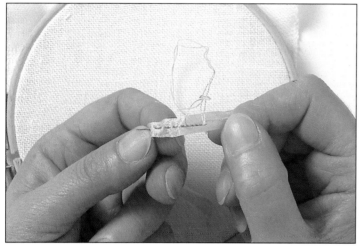

This stitch is very suitable for making charming little roses. Just one ribbon 7 mm wide may be used for each flower or an additional, smaller ribbon of another color. About 4–6" (10–15 cm) of ribbon is required on average, so left over strips can be used. When two colors are employed, lay the smaller one over the bigger one, being sure to keep the borders in line.

Knot the ends of the two ribbons together. With the same colored thread, baste a small line in the center.

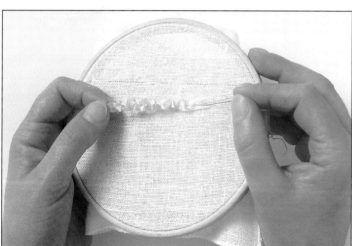

Pull the thread slightly until it forms a ruck. Ruck into a round and with small stitches sew the ends to form a circle.

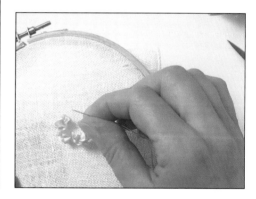

Apply the rose to the fabric with small stitches.

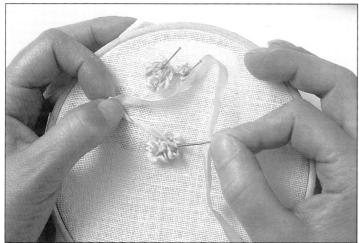

Lastly, embroider a knotted stitch in the center of the flower.

ROSE STITCH

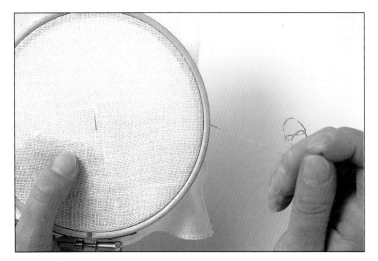

Make a base with mouliné thread the same color as the ribbon. Make a traditional knot, bring the needle out to the front of the work, making a flat stitch.

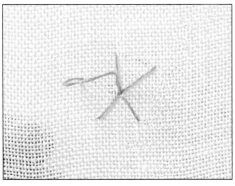

Embroider a four-pointed star with two mouliné embroidery threads matching the ribbon color.

Turn the work over and fasten the thread well on the back. The stability of the rose depends on this preparatory work.

This small rose, constructed on a web of mouliné threads, is attractive and decorative.

This embroidery can be done on any kind of fabric as it is well secured to the fabric thanks to the threaded base. It is very suitable therefore for shoes, trousers, bags, hats, etc.

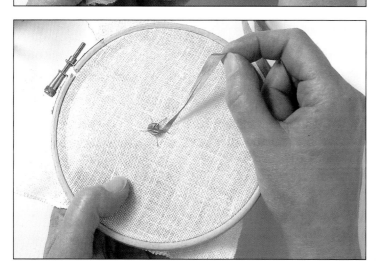

Now take the ribbon, make a flat stitch and bring the needle out to the front of the work, in the center of the star.

Pass the needle under the first stitch and fasten the second stitch.

Continue by passing the needle alternately under and over the star sides. Make sure the ribbon is not too taut so that the rose remains soft.

Work in circles until the sides in cotton are completely covered. Then bring the ribbon to the back and fasten off. Two ribbons of contrasting colors may also be used to make this rose.

BOW RIBBON STITCH

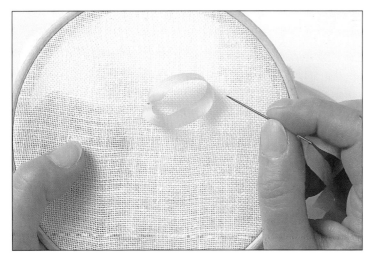

The front of the work make a large loop on the right. Then bring the needle to the back. To the front make another loop on the left. Bring the needle to the back of the work.

Bring the needle out to the front between the two loops. Embroider a straight stitch starting from the top downwards and keep it a little slack. Bring the needle to the back.

Repeat on the other side of the bow, leaving the loop longer, then bring the ribbon to the back. Bring the needle out from the center and make a fastening stitch to shape the knot.

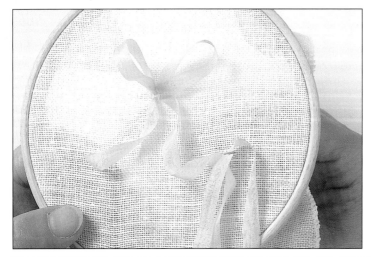

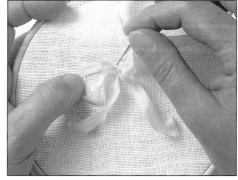

This very decorative ribbon may be used to decorate the corners of cushions, blouse pockets, baby sheets and a host of other objects. There is no limit as to the width of the silk ribbon to be used.

Model the two loops, giving them some shape and pin them down. Make small, knotted stitches to keep the ribbon in shape, then remove the pins. Fasten off on the back.

ROSES

ROSE: THE WORLD'S FLOWER

The rose is known to everybody as the "Queen of flowers." It is certainly the most popular and sought after flower in the world. A red rose means LOVE the world over. Tradition has it that roses transmit different messages according to their color: most of these messages are positive and romantic, but some are contradictory and even negative, therefore take care when choosing a bunch of roses to give as a gift.

Yellow roses imply worn-out love and jealousy.
Moss roses indicate pride.
Cabbage rose is the ambassador of love; this is why it was so popular in Victorian times on St. Valentine cards.
It must not be forgotten that the rose is typical of the month of May, the month of weddings. For this reason, weddings, roses, and affairs of the heart have, with the passing of time, come to be considered insolubly linked together.

ROSE BUDS

Rose buds transmit messages of youth and pure beauty; this is why a bride's bouquet is traditionally made up of rose buds.

Ribbon roses are easy to make and are a perfect decoration both for wedding dresses and refined gift-wraps.

Roses can be made with most types of ribbon: satin in particular makes filmy roses, suitable for embellishing every corner of the house, while voile is perfect for making beautiful, romantic cabbage roses; a beautiful "silk effect" is achieved by using two different shades of color.

The instructions outlined in the following pages will help you indulge your fancy in making open, filmy buds or roses of different colors, sizes and texture, as well as teach you how to make stems with an iron wire covered in gutta-percha and how to bunch them together into delightful compositions, bouquets, wreaths to use on special occasions.

Fold the end of the ribbon on the inside, leaving a couple of inches free to use as a handhold.

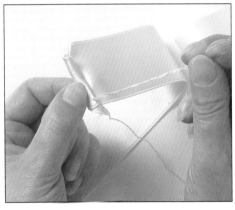

Roll the doubled ribbon a couple of times on itself to form a small tube.

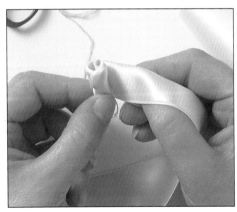

Keep the ribbon slightly slack. Insert a needle with a matching color.

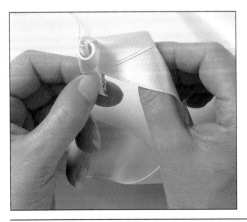

Start to fasten the central part with a needle and thread.

Fold the ribbon at an angle on the outside and roll it on itself, securing it with a stitch.

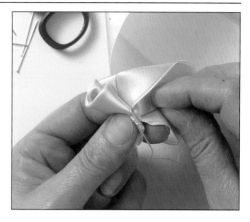

Before proceeding with a new fold, slacken the ribbon a little and begin again, by making a right angle towards the outside. Roll the ribbon on itself once more, keeping it tight, and fasten well.

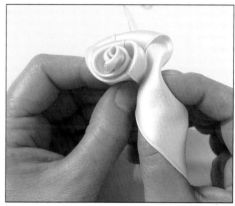

Proceed in this manner until you have reached the size desired.

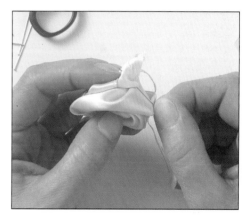

You can now admire your finished rose.

A FLOWERY TABLE

We have the habit of decorating our home with great care on special occasions, so why not give a new touch to our table too? You can embellish your traditional white tablecloth with a "cascade" of filmy roses lying on fresh or synthetic ivy shoots.

To makes these roses you will need about 8–10" (20–25 cm) of satin ribbon with a framework (metal wire around the edges.) Make a sufficient number of roses, secure them to the shoots with bi-adhesive tape, and group them together to make a cascade, alternating shapes and colors at your heart's desire.

In the same manner, make small bouquets to use as place markers, or bunches of roses to put in vases with which to decorate your table. Buds scattered here and there add a touch of elegance to the ensemble.

STEMMED ROSES

– Procure a metal wire like those used by florists and make a noose at one end.
– Insert a thin zinc wire 5/32" (0.40 mm) into the noose, twisting it well. It will come in handy in subsequent work phases.
– Cover the noose with ribbon of the width desired.
– To make the center of the rose, wrap the ribbon around the noose a couple of times. Give the zinc wire a couple of turns to secure the ribbon.

– Once again fold the ribbon at an angle and wrap it around the center, making a soft petal. Secure it with the wire and proceed in this manner until you reach the size desired.
– To make the stem, wrap the metal wire with gutta-percha. Gradually add the leaves, arranging them as the fancy strikes you.
– After having made several roses, bunch them together to create delightful compositions.

GARLANDS

YOU WILL NEED

- *a wreath about 8 and 13/16" (22 cm) wide*
- *ivory ribbon 128" (320 cm) long*
- *lace ribbon 68" (170 cm) long*
- *pins*
- *ribbons of various widths and colors*

The tradition of decorating homes with garlands goes way back long before the advent of Christianity. For many pagan peoples, the winter solstice marked the end of the year and the coming of spring. They would use evergreens, the symbol of fertility and regeneration, to decorate garlands. In December, the Romans used to adorn their home with garlands and wreaths. A feast was dedicated to the Goddess of Health, which lasted several days, During the feast, garlands decorated with plants and ribbons were exchanged. These garlands, attached to the door, ensured health for the coming year. This tradition has remained unaltered throughout the centuries and is still in use today.

- Bind the garland entirely with the ivory-colored satin ribbon.
- Secure it to the garland with pins and then cut off any excess ribbon.
- Proceed by wrapping the lace ribbon around the garland, making sure it is sufficiently spaced out so that the sheen of the underlying satin ribbon can be seen.
- Pin a group of pre-prepared roses and complete the decoration with delicate little bows.

A beautiful garland looks perfect in every corner of the home: it can be hung on the entrance door to welcome guests, used as a Christmas decoration, or in attractive compositions like those made with candles.

HATS AND BAGS

YOU WILL NEED

- velvet
- lining
- cords for the shoulder straps
- satin and silk ribbons
- straw hats
- needle and thread
- stick glue

Simple straw hats adorned with small roses acquire an elegant tone and are transformed in to hats, which can be shown off at important ceremonies.

The handbags are no longer accessories suitable for the evenings only, but have come to be an integral part of our everyday wear, thanks also to many fashion designers who have brought them back into fashion: a touch of madness which could be used even when wearing jeans.

This original cloth bag was made in black silk crepe. Cut a disk about 2 and 7/16–3 and 3/18" (6–8 cm) wide and sew a rectangle about 12–14" (30–35 cm) high around it. Sew two seams at 2 and 7/16–3" (6–7 cm) from the border and insert a cord (in this case the cord is made of beads). To the front of the bag, sew a bouquet of roses.

MORE IDEAS WITH ROSES

YOU WILL NEED

- velvet
- shoes from Friuli
- silk ribbons
- needle and thread
- lining

A tiny but extravagant idea for a waistcoat: a bouquet of flowers embroidered with silk ribbons, buds and softly shaded leaves; suitable for wearing over a sheath dress, perfect over a white blouse and trousers.

Traditional slippers take on a new and romantic air if embroidered with roses in warm pink hues.

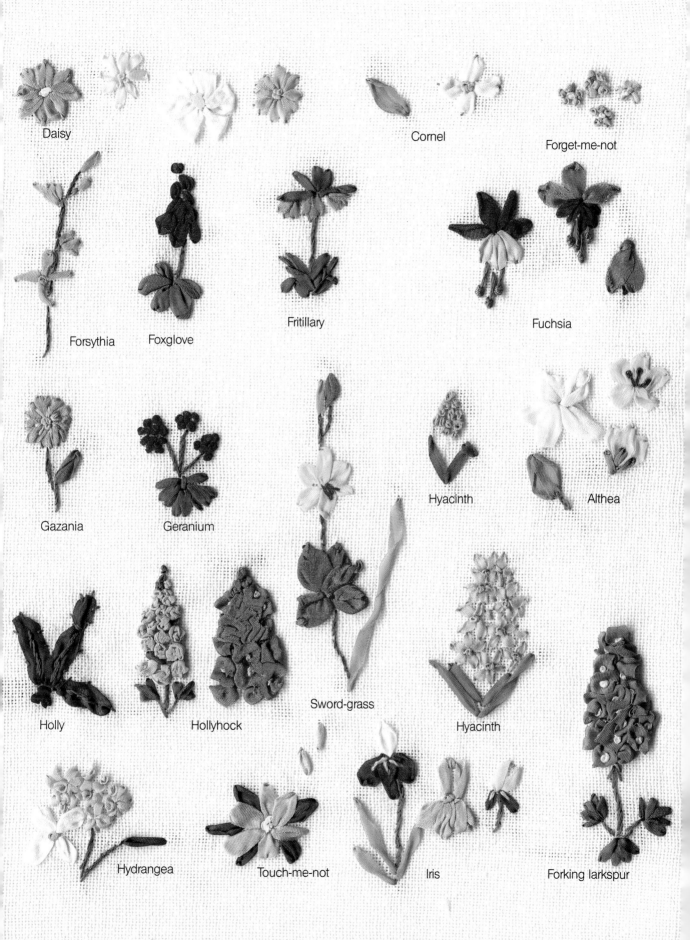

Daisy

Cornel

Forget-me-not

Forsythia

Foxglove

Fritillary

Fuchsia

Gazania

Geranium

Hyacinth

Althea

Holly

Hollyhock

Sword-grass

Hyacinth

Hydrangea

Touch-me-not

Iris

Forking larkspur

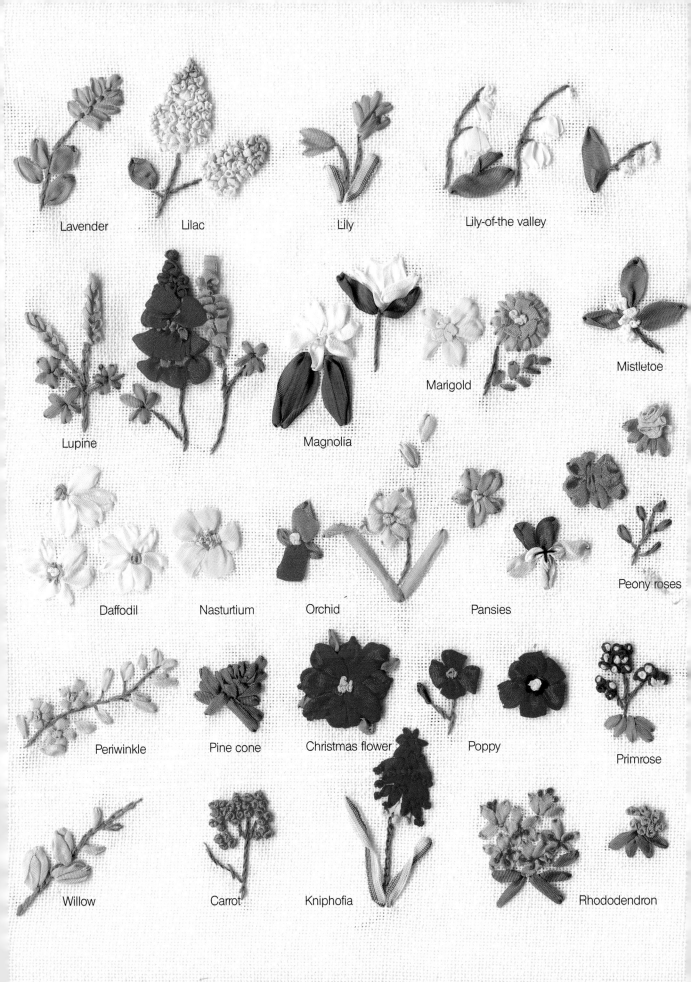

Lavender

Lilac

Lily

Lily-of-the valley

Lupine

Magnolia

Marigold

Mistletoe

Daffodil

Nasturtium

Orchid

Pansies

Peony roses

Periwinkle

Pine cone

Christmas flower

Poppy

Primrose

Willow

Carrot

Kniphofia

Rhododendron

PANSIES

PANSIES—THE FLOWERS OF THE YEAR

Pansies bloom in such abundance
and for so long that they wear out
and die, therefore it is necessary
to grow them every year
starting from the seed.
Pansies originally
came from England.
The tender "tricolor"
violet is always
depicted in pictures
of spring. No garden
can be complete
without some pansies.
Even during the winter they
can give special joy to
those who know
how to grow them.

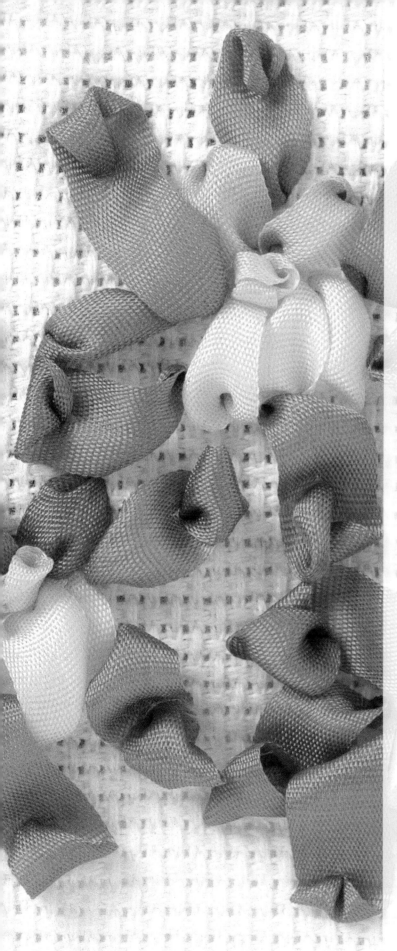

Pansies too have their story with roots in legend. Legend in fact has it that Cupid shot an arrow towards a simple wild pansy. The wound caused by the arrow changed the flower's color from white to violet, as Oberon describes in the play *A Midsummer Night's dream* by William Shakespeare:

That very time I saw, but thou couldst not
Flying between the cold moon and the earth,
Cupid all arm'd: a certain aim he took
At a fair vestal throned by the west,
And loosed his love-shaft smartly from his bow,
As it should pierce a hundred thousand hearts:
But I might see young Cupid's fiery shaft
Quench'd in the chaste beams of the watery moon,
And the imperial votaress passed on,
In maiden meditation, fancy-free.
Yet mark'd I where the bolt of Cupid fell:
It fell upon a little western flower,
Before milk-white, now purple with love's wound
And maidens call it love in idleness.

MORE PANSIES

After having basted the stomacher to be embroidered on a piece of fabric, insert it into the frame in order to have a rigid support.

Bring the needle to the front of the work and make a free-standing loop. When the loop is the desired length, fasten it to the fabric with a pin. Bring the ribbon to the back.

Return to the front once more, make two more loops at the side of the central loop, and fasten both with pins. Bring the ribbon to the back again and fasten well.

Change color and make a straight stitch on the right and another on the left of the desired length, thus forming two small, slack ears above the first three loops.

With the dark embroidery thread make small stitches above the first three loops to make realistic looking pistils.

Insert a knotted stitch of a warm yellow color in the center of the pansy. Your flower is now finished.

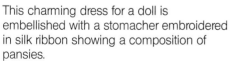

This charming dress for a doll is embellished with a stomacher embroidered in silk ribbon showing a composition of pansies.

Enrich your favorite recipes book with a cover made from the same material as your tablecloth. Sew the word Recipes on with braid and surround it with delicate pansies.

CELEBRATING WITH PANSIES

Thousands of pansies shower onto this spring tablecloth, some of them printed on the fabric, others embroidered in silk to embellish both the table-cloth and the objects shown.

YOU WILL NEED

For the labels:
- *Aida cloth 6" (15 cm)*
- *braid 22" (55 cm)*
- *violet colored ribbon 1m*
- *embroidery ribbons*

Here is a bag for holding bread with an embroidered label. To make it, get some patterned cotton measuring 32 x 14" (80 x 35 cm). Place the label where desired and decorate it with violet braid. The writing on the label was done in cross-stitch with shaded moulinè cotton. The flowers were made with 9/32" (7 mm) ribbons, as were the leaves. Here, delicate pansies were embroidered, to match the fabric. To make the bag, fold the fabric in half and sew along the two sides on the wrong side. Turn the right side out and fold 2" (5 cm) of fabric inwards along the open edge to form the border. Sew two seams a few cm from each other into which insert the fastening ribbon.

Here are some cheerful bags for holding just about everything, in various shapes and sizes. They are very handy and very easy and satisfying to make. You can let your imagination run wild when choosing the fabrics. Cut them out and make them up without difficulty and finish them off with embroidery and ribbons. So you'll have a small stockings-holder or handkerchief-holder for a young, romantic girl's birthday or a useful and attractive present for every occasion.

PHOTO ALBUM AND GREETING CARDS

This photo album has been created with hand-made paper where small fragments of pansy petals can be seen in relief. The strip in Aida cloth has also been embroidered in silk with pansies in the classical yellow and purple of this flower. Small green leaves surround them and a line of cross-stitch embroidered in silk finishes off the work. This is an idea for an original gift, suitable for a person of refined taste.

YOU WILL NEED

- *a photo album*
- *a strip of Aida cloth*
- *silk ribbons of various widths*
- *greeting cards of different sizes*

These unusual cards created with hand-made paper have an inserted central piece of Aida cloth, embroidered with pansies and field flowers. The originality and the refined decoration make them ideal for sending good wishes at important moments such as weddings and births. They also look extremely well as place markers.

PROJECTS

DECORATING THE TABLE

YOU WILL NEED

- *jacquard fabric 58 x 48" (160 x 120 cm)*
- *lace 2 and 10/32" (5.80 cm)*
- *two strips of Aida cloth about 32" (80 cm) each*
- *colored silk ribbons*
- *thread*
- *ivy shoots for decorating*
- *daisies, roses, sunflowers*
- *rustic basket*

This beautiful white jacquard tablecloth has been embellished with large strips of Aida cloth, on which bunches of multicolored silk flowers were embroidered, as well as with lace borders. The ensemble is enhanced by the sunflower cloth underneath.

Snow-white daisies and roses embroidered with silk ribbons emerge from a very original vase. Made with different damask fabrics assembled to make a delightful patchwork in warm yellow hues, this vase is set off by large silk-embroidered daisies. This is an original idea for flowers that will never wither.

This picture shows a close-up of the silk ribbon embroidery enhancing the tablecloth. The wide variety of flowers, worked and assembled with great skill, creates color patches which are extremely pleasant to the eye and which stand out against the white background of the Aida cloth.

Silk ribbon can be washed and ironed, one more reason for proposing this tablecloth of such rich embroidery. It is always advisable to iron the embroidery on the back. Should it flatten, wet the ribbon only. As soon as it dries, the embroidery will immediately regain its filmy shape. Silk ribbons can be bleached slightly.

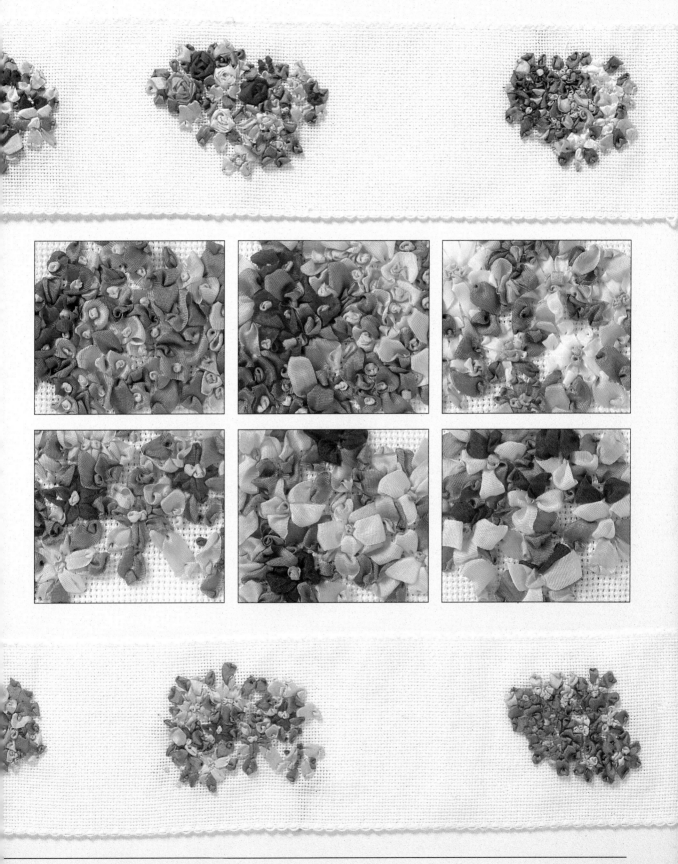

FOR THE
BATHROOM

In the last few years we have witnessed a growing interest in the bathroom, with more and more importance being attached to its structure, furnishing and accessories. So why not embellish this room further and make it even more welcoming and personalized? Let's start with the linen: linen, cotton or damask towels can be enriched and personalized with delicate motifs or by letters embroidered in silk ribbon.

- silk ribbons of 9/32–3/32"
  (7 and 3 mm) in different colors
- single or two-thread mouliné
  thread

Draw the letter with a tracing pencil and then transfer it to the fabric. This letter shows us a fine example of couching. Begin the embroidery from the top, making the first flower, then continue down with roses, daisies and leaves, alternating shapes and colors in an attractive way.

To embroider the letter 'B,' first, outline the base with the twisted stitch using mouliné thread and then make the flowers using colored silk ribbon. Always begin from the top so as to create a colorful cascade.

Also for the letter 'P' embroider the outline with the twisted stitch using mouliné thread, and then the daisies and leaves with silk ribbon, alternating colors.

Begin from the bottom, on the right side of the letter, first making a rose, then a daisy with the fern stitch and subsequently other flowers until you reach the end of the letter, which is embroidered with the twisted stitch using mouliné thread.

These towels in light-blue and pink damask linen are embroidered with a delicate frieze of flowers and leaves worked with a 3/32" (3 mm) long ribbon. Roses were chosen as a decoration for the light-blue towel, while daisies and wild flowers were used to adorn the pink one.

On this pink towel, a shoot of fuchsia is enriched with cross-stitch leaves.

This balsa box gains value with this composition of roses made with the zigzag technique, complete with pistils and green leaves. The composition, applied with hot glue to the lid, was finished with a large bow in the same color modeled directly onto the box. It is an amusing idea to use as soap dish or as a make-up bag.

On these white honeycomb towels, the frieze, embroidered with silk ribbon using the cross-stitch, is interspersed with roses and leaves.

This rose sewn together with its bud makes a delightful hair clasp.

The elegance of these towels in damask linen, embroidered with delicate motifs, makes them particularly suitable for a wedding gift or an important anniversary. In the garland-shaped decoration, roses are worked with a 9/32" (7 mm) long ribbon. By holding the ribbon tight, buds are formed. The leaves are embroidered with the lazy daisy stitch while the decorated loop stitch closes the garland. The work is finished off with a knotted stitch. The embroideries embellishing the towels depicted on the next page, finished off with lace applications, present roses worked with the same ribbon and technique, but kept very slack. This simple touch is enough to give a different effect to our work.

YOU WILL NEED

Ribbons
- *roses 20" (50 cm) each*
- *dark green leaves 44" (110 cm)*
- *light green leaves 32" (80 cm)*

Position the motif to be embroidered on the towel, then make the three roses of whatever color you choose. Now embroider the leaves in the two different shades of green all around the flowers.

IN THE KITCHEN

Once the kitchen was considered the undisputed territory of the lady of the house, today the kitchen has become the reign of the whole family, a welcoming room which is being used more and more frequently not only as the place where meals are consumed, but also where to meet friends with whom to exchange opinions or play a card game after dinner. This is one more reason for embellishing it with a series of original and elegant accessories. Attractive embroidered dishcloths, for example, can be a truly useful and amusing idea for giving color to the room or for enlivening breakfast. By using the various techniques available and choosing theme motifs according to the season, delightful combinations can be made On these kitchen cloths, printed with designs reminiscent of the garden, lots of colored vegetables can be seen on the border of the Aida cloth.

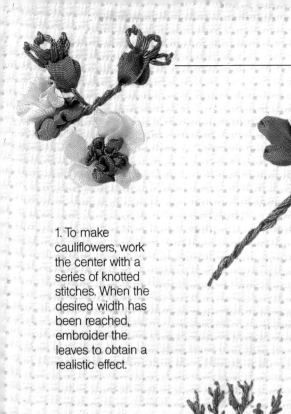

1. To make cauliflowers, work the center with a series of knotted stitches. When the desired width has been reached, embroider the leaves to obtain a realistic effect.

2. To make the sprig of red currants embroider the base of the branch in twisted stitch with embroidery thread. Make the leaves with medium sized green ribbon, keeping the ribbon slack all the time. For the berries make a series of knotted stitches arranged in a bunch, then go over them with the 9/32" (7 mm) ribbon using a straight stitch When the work is finished embroider a knotted stitch with brown mouliné thread at the base of the fruit.

3. To make the carrots sew a series of little stitches to give volume and a raised effect, then make a straight stitch to cover all.

Finish with the roots, worked in twisted stitches with mouliné thread. The leaves can also be made with ribbons.

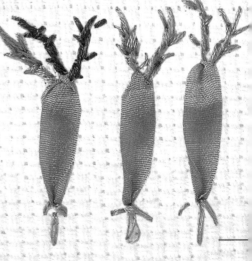

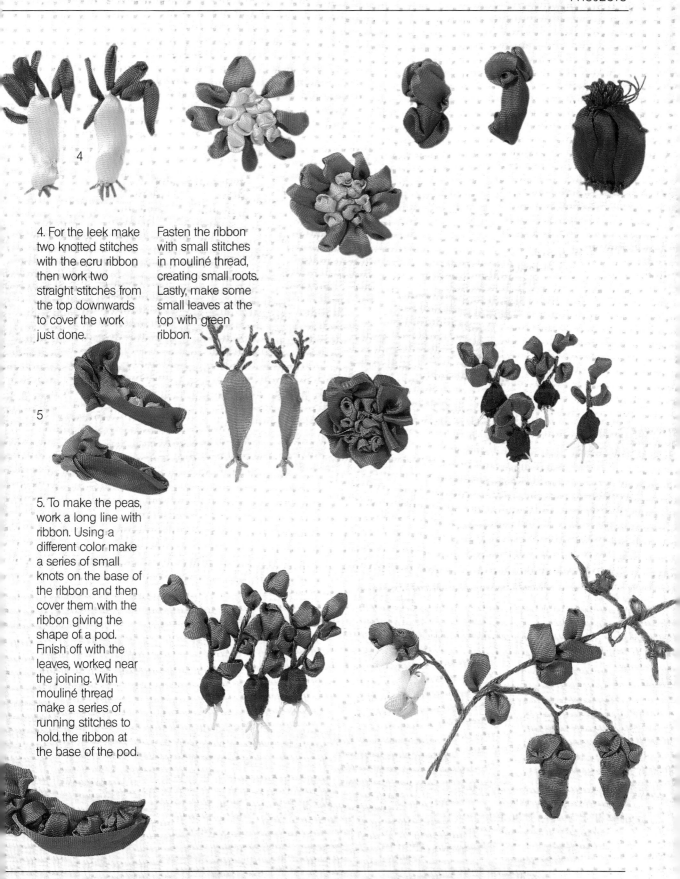

4. For the leek make two knotted stitches with the ecru ribbon then work two straight stitches from the top downwards to cover the work just done.

Fasten the ribbon with small stitches in mouliné thread, creating small roots. Lastly, make some small leaves at the top with green ribbon.

5. To make the peas, work a long line with ribbon. Using a different color make a series of small knots on the base of the ribbon and then cover them with the ribbon giving the shape of a pod. Finish off with the leaves, worked near the joining. With mouliné thread make a series of running stitches to hold the ribbon at the base of the pod.

CAKE CAGE

The traditional cages for protection against insects,
normally used in the country to preserve food, have
come back into fashion today for eating out of doors.
They are easily available in shops with household
goods and can be touched up to give an elegant
effect to the table. To embroider them just open
the cage. The iron rods keep the fabric taut
and make embroidering easy. Work the
motifs of your choice and finish off with lace
sewn on with small, hidden stitches.
This could be an attractive gift for a friend
who likes organizing meals outdoors, or
for a picnic during the summer
months

APRONS

A nice overall apron is ideal when making the last hurried preparations for friends arriving for dinner.

This butcher's apron, in heavy pink and white checked cotton, has a handy hold all pocket cut on the bias. A medallion of roses in silk, surrounded by small leaves, is embroidered on the upper part.

A heart of yellow and orange daisies decorates the upper part in Aida cloth of this check apron. A full frill cut on the bias finishes off the bottom edge, giving the whole a romantic look.

This overall with its warm golden, red and fawn coloring has a somewhat Christmas look. Made from American cotton, it has a border in contrasting fabric the same as that used for the diamond shaped patches and the square on the upper part. This latter, of red Aida cloth, is embroidered in silk ribbon with Christmas flowers and holly leaves.

This attractive overall in green seersucker is enriched at the waist with a green strip which ties at the back. The same type borders the upper part, which is worked with small flowers gathered in a bright yellow bow.

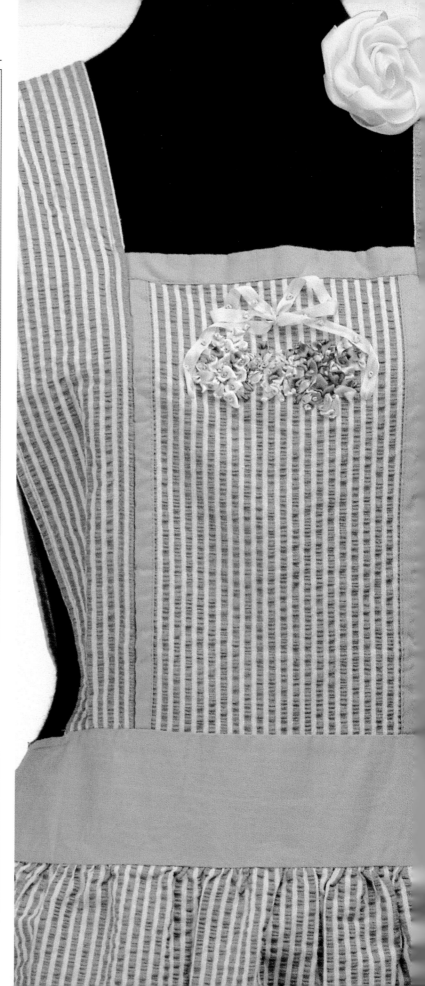

RECIPE BOOK

This is an amusing way of collecting and keeping your tastiest recipes in order. Get hold of a rigid diary and cover it with a patterned fabric. Embroider a tag in Aida cloth with silk ribbon, using the lazy daisy stitch, and decorate it with red corals. Glue the tag on the cover with a film of vinyl glue, then finish it along the borders with braid.

These potholders are two squares crocheted and doubled in lamé thread. Once you have reached the length desired, about 4 and 13/16" (12 cm), embroider with silk ribbon, choose motifs which strike your fancy (in this case a luminous Christmas flower). Overlap the two squares to obtain greater thickness and finish the potholder with a small loop for hanging purposes. Finish off the borders with a ribbon of the same color, tying it with a delightful little bow.

More ideas for the home. These hearts were made with lamé thread and a medley of crocheted stitches, arches and chains. In the center is an open rose enhanced by a ribbon of the same color that is tied at the top into a bow. These are suitable as lavender or soap holders for the bathroom or, filled with wadding, as a pincushion.

BLANKET

This warm plaid in ecru wool is enriched with delicate flower compositions embroidered with silk ribbon. Suitable for baby cots or prams, it can be a delightful idea to give as a present to mothers or friends with romantic tastes. This demonstrates to what extent silk ribbon is versatile and suitable for all types and textures of fabrics and objects.

This elegant bag is in chinz bordered with a cord in warm pink hues and embellished by two large satin bows of the same color. An amusing idea for putting a plaid away!

Find the center of the squares and embroider your favorite flowers, singles or small bunches of daisies, small garlands, being sure to alternate the colors. A bead can be inserted into the center of the daisies.

NIGHT GOWN

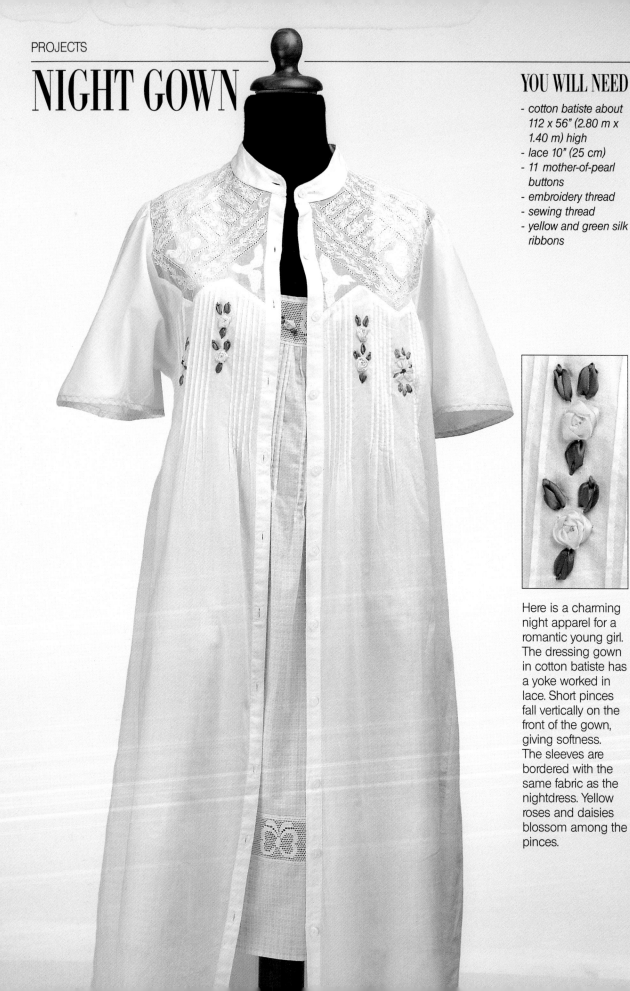

YOU WILL NEED

- cotton batiste about
  112 x 56" (2.80 m x
  1.40 m) high
- lace 10" (25 cm)
- 11 mother-of-pearl
  buttons
- embroidery thread
- sewing thread
- yellow and green silk
  ribbons

Here is a charming
night apparel for a
romantic young girl.
The dressing gown
in cotton batiste has
a yoke worked in
lace. Short pinces
fall vertically on the
front of the gown,
giving softness.
The sleeves are
bordered with the
same fabric as the
nightdress. Yellow
roses and daisies
blossom among the
pinces.

YOU WILL NEED

- *tartan 68 x 44"*
  (1.70 m x 1.10 m)
- *lace 120 x 2.2"*
  (3 m x 5.5 cm)
- *sewing thread*
- *yellow and green silk*
  ribbons

The shoulder straps, yoke and insert of this cool nightdress in yellow tartan are made in macramé lace with love knots. The same roses embroidered on the dressing gown are embroidered this nightdress.

NIGHTDRESS

This white linen nightdress sports an original neckline held by a contrasting ribbon adorned with two sewn roses. Small bunches of flowers embroidered on the front embellish the ensemble.

MORNING GOWN

If you find an old morning gown in grandma's trunk, so why not transform it into a fashionable item of clothing to be worn in your relaxed moments? Small roses bordered with small leaves are embroidered on the front. Old buttons assume a new life: small roses made with the rucked running stitch are applied with tiny stitches on the old button. This idea can also be applied to your every day blouse.

FLOWERY DRESSES

YOU WILL NEED

- *patterned calico 57 x 44" (1.50 m x 1.10 m)*
- *Hardanger cloth 16" (40 cm)*
- *different-colored ribbons of various widths*
- *white bias binding for the hem*

A delightful city dress, with a skirt in summer calico and bodice in ecru Hardanger cloth embroidered in silk ribbon with vivid multicolored flowers.
Those of you who do not own a sewing machine can easily hand-make this dress. Cut two pieces of fabric about 30" (75 cm) wide, sew them together and ruck them on the upper part. Cut out the fabric for the bodice and border it on the back with the bias binding. Sew the embroidered bodice to the skirt, completing it with the hem. Finish off with an ecru rose applied on the shoulder strap.

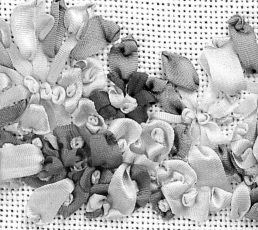

Cool dress in checked white batiste tone on tone. The sleeveless bodice has a deep neckline, embellished with silk ribbon embroidery in warm summer hues and a white bow.

SUMMER DRESS

Sunny summer clothes in fresh calico to wear both in the city and at the sea. Mother and daughter wear the same dress: the only variation lies in the embroidery. On the girl's dress, a cat seems to be looking at a swarm of bees and ladybirds dance on the flowers which blossom from behind the fence. On the mother's dress a house is enclosed among blossoming trees and creepers. On the surrounding meadow, the linen is hanging out to dry in the wind. Among the flowery hills we glimpse a village with its church. These embroideries, seemingly elaborate, can be carried out easily using the various techniques acquired up to now.

YOU WILL NEED

FOR THE GIRL
- *yellow Aida cloth for the bodice*
- *check fabric 16" (40 cm)*
- *patterned fabric 32" (80 cm)*
- *dotted fabric 30" (75 cm)*
- *braid 280" (7 m)*
- *tailor's chalk*
- *pins*
- *thread*
- *zip 12" (30 cm)*

The measurements given include the seams.
Try out the model first in paper, to get the size required right. Cut two pieces of fabric measuring 8" (20 cm) each from the check fabric and ruck until you have a strip 56" (140 cm) long. From the second patterned cloth first cut the back of the bodice, then the two sleeves and lastly the collar on the bias. Then cut two strips 8" (20 cm) long and ruck until the strip is 88" (2.20 m) long. Now cut three strips 9 and 3/16" (23 cm) long and ruck until you get to 128" (3.20 m). Embroider the bodice as your fancy strikes you. Assemble the bodice, front and back, the sleeves, the collar, and the flounces and apply braid over the seams. With any fabric left over, you can make a miniature dress to use as a pincushion.

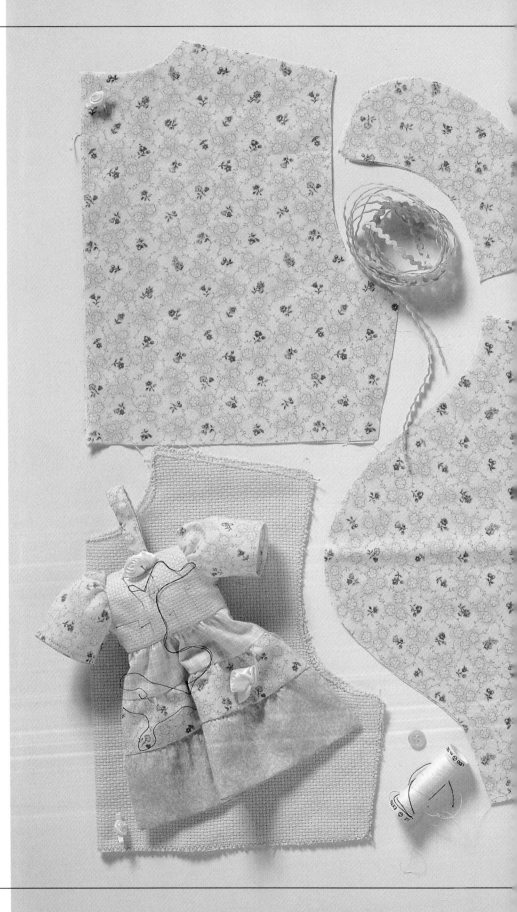

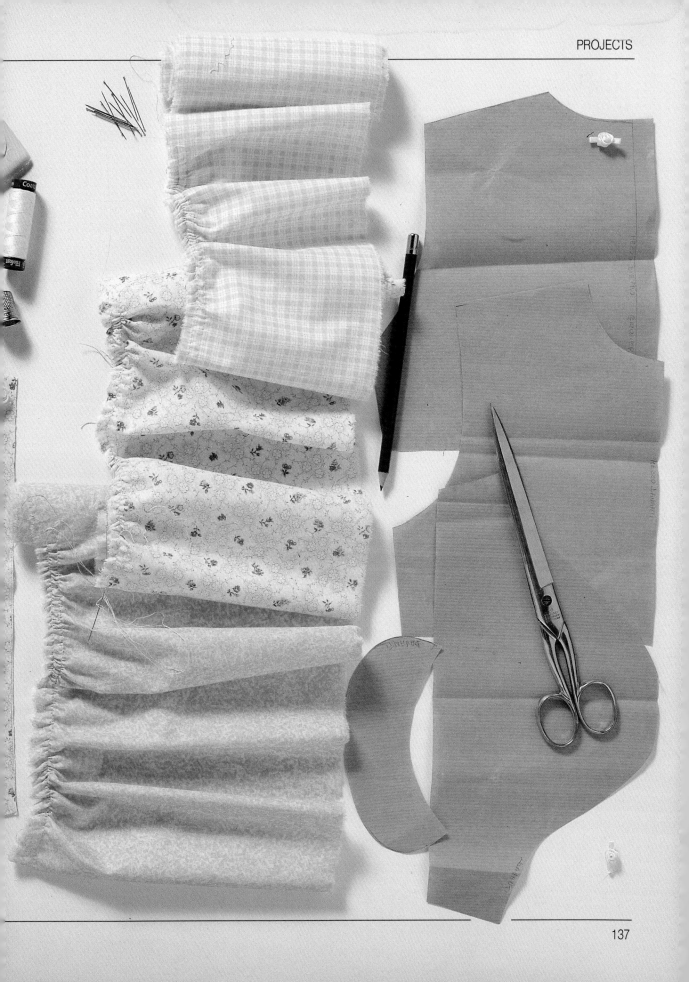

BAGS

Two bags made of embroidered fabric, suitable for a walk with friends or for shopping.

YOU WILL NEED

First model
- *various furnishing material*
- *braid*
- *gold hearts*
- *large heart in mother-of-pearl*
- *lining of the same color*
- *silk ribbons*

Second model
- *various worked damascene material*
- *cords*
- *bows*
- *braid*
- *beads and crystals*
- *silk ribbons*
- *lining and padding*
- *zip*

The first model, in patchwork, measures 12 x 16" (30 x 40 cm). Choose furnishing materials of different patterns, cut out squares of various shapes and sizes and assemble to your taste. Embroider some squares with your favorite motifs, decorate others with small gold hearts and a large heart in mother-of-pearl adorned with a bow. Once the embroidery is finished, sew the lining with small hidden stitches. The handles are made with the same braid as that used for the trimmings.

The second model, made with yellow damask, is fitted with large cord handles and multicolored bows. It measures 12 x 16" (30 x 40 cm). Use various remnants of material for the front. For the back and the sides, use a padded fabric. After having assembled the various pieces, start embroidering: here you can really let your imagination run wild in terms of colors and stitches. When the embroidery is finished, enhance with beads the arabesques of the fabric and sew them on the pre-drawn lines. To make your work even more precious add glass beads and embellish the ensemble with crystals.

CLOTH BAGS

This is yet another original idea for a personalized gift. Delightful all-purpose embroidered cloth bags are ideal for holding our mobile phone, make-up or keys.

These bags are made of velvet or heavy silk furnishing material with delightful floral motifs, some of which are here shown enlarged, embroidered in silk ribbons and organdie. Some are finished off with silk cords, but all have a rucked slot for closing, either with a ribbon or a cord.

YOU WILL NEED

- *silk velvet in various colors*
- *decorative ribbons*
- *silk ribbons for embroidering*
- *matching cords*
- *bows or gold beads*

Cut out a rectangle of velvet fabric 12" (30 cm) long and 10" (25 cm) wide. Embroider the central part towards the bottom using the frame to avoid flattening the fabric. Sew a central seam; ruck with some heavy thread the bottom part of the fabric, from the back. Make a double border on the top part of the bag, sew and fill as you wish. Close by rucking the opening with a colored ribbon, and tie a filmy bow.

More colored bags, this time in miniature! They can be used instead of bows in key cases. Filled with potpourri, they perfume rooms. Replete with chocolates and sweets, they make original place markers for an important dinner or amusing gifts during an evening with friends.

143

PICTURES AND FRAMES

YOU WILL NEED

- *linen cloth*
- *sheet polystyrene*
- *cord*
- *pins and glue*

Here is a welcome gift for a new home: Home sweet home. Two phrases of good wishes embroidered in cross-stitch on white and light-blue linen and embellished with various silk ribbon embroidery stitches. Having completed the plaque with the motifs and stitches most congenial to you, cut out a sheet of polystyrene of the same size. Place it under the piece of fabric making sure the borders coincide and, with the help of pins, keep it well taut. On the back carefully glue a sheet of paper to hide the background. Finish off with a two-color silk cord around the borders.

YOU WILL NEED

- *12" (30 cm) of silk moiré fabric*
- *cards*
- *bookbinding fabric with the same color as the ribbons*
- *vinyl glue*
- *cords*

Here are two original and precious embroidered frames in which to place your most cherished photographs. Cut an oval or a heart shape on a piece of card, then line it with embroidered fabric, having first made a series of cuts on the back so that the fabric remains taut and does not crease. Dilute some vinyl glue in water and glue the binding fabric on to the second card, both front and back. Leave to dry, then assemble the two cards, making sure to leave one side open in which to insert the photograph. Fit the borders with a two-color silk cord.

IDEAS FOR PRESENTS

Initials are a recurring motif, which are always appreciated no matter how they've been embroidered. So why not embroider a sampler, where a myriad of multicolored flowers and easy stitches embellish your initials or those of a person dear to you?

For a friend who loves reading, here is a gift that will be greatly appreciated. This delightful bookmark is easily made by gluing a silk rectangle, on which three colored roses blossom, on a piece of card. The embroidery is enhanced by a frame made with the running stitch.

This small bouquet of flowers is enclosed in a cross-stitch frame. A large silk ribbon of the same color, with elaborate loops at the edges, decorates and finishes off the frame.

PROJECTS

PATTERNED BOXES

Round, rectangular, square... boxes of every shape,
color and texture delightfully embroidered with silk
ribbons, can become an elegant furnishing
accessory that goes beyond their original function.
It is up to you and your imagination to find where
to put them in your home: in the bathroom,
as perfumed soap dishes for your guests, in the
bedroom as a jewel casket or a make-up holder.
They have always been a greatly appreciated gift,
especially if replete with sweets or chocolates.

DECORATING THE CLOSET

How many times, on opening a wardrobe, are we faced with small objects, neatly stacked away, which remind us of past events dear to our 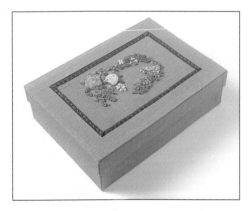 memory! And here is a small peaked cap sported during our first bicycle rides on lovely spring days.

These beautiful boxes coated in green satin and trimmed with braid and cord, given by friends for birthdays, have become practical containers for letters and postcards. And again, towels and cushions enriched with elaborate embroideries.

A cascade of multicolored flowers enliven these cushions in romantic white linen, trimmed with lace and ribbons. They are perfect for a young girl's bedroom.

PERFUMED DOLLS

Perfumed bags, extremely useful for wardrobes and drawers, are here proposed in a truly unusual shape: pretty little "dolls" dressed to the nines with fresh dresses in patterned cotton and bodice in Aida cloth embroidered with silk ribbon. These objects are made with such care and skill that they are beautiful in themselves, and this is why they can always be included in the list of most appreciated gifts.

Made in silver and gold, they make original wedding keepsakes for silver or golden weddings.

You could choose these attractive dolls to try out your first steps at ribbon embroidery: on a small piece of fabric, you have the opportunity of trying your hand at making these small flowers and getting the knack so that you can then move on to more complex projects.

YOU WILL NEED

- 8" (20 cm) patterned
  fabric
- satin or Aida cloth for
  the bodice
- colored silk ribbons
- needle and thread
- pins

To make this doll-
shaped sachet, you
can use the paper
model depicted on
this page. Sew the
top part of the
bodice inserting the
pre-prepared loop.
Hem the sleeves,
rucking them at the
top, and apply
keeping the bodice
open. Close the
sides of the bodice
and sleeves. Sew
the sides and the
end part of the skirt,
leaving 3 and 3/16"
(8 cm) open at the
top on one side
only. Ruck the skirt
and sew it with
small stitches to the
bodice.

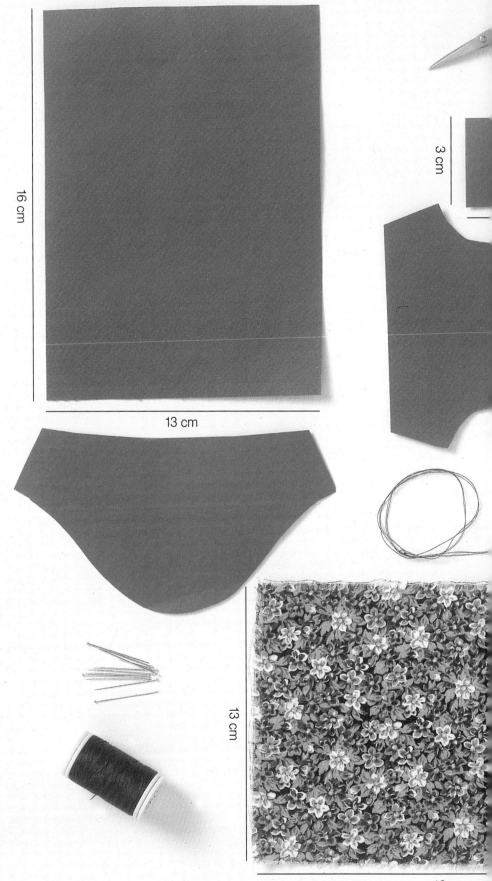

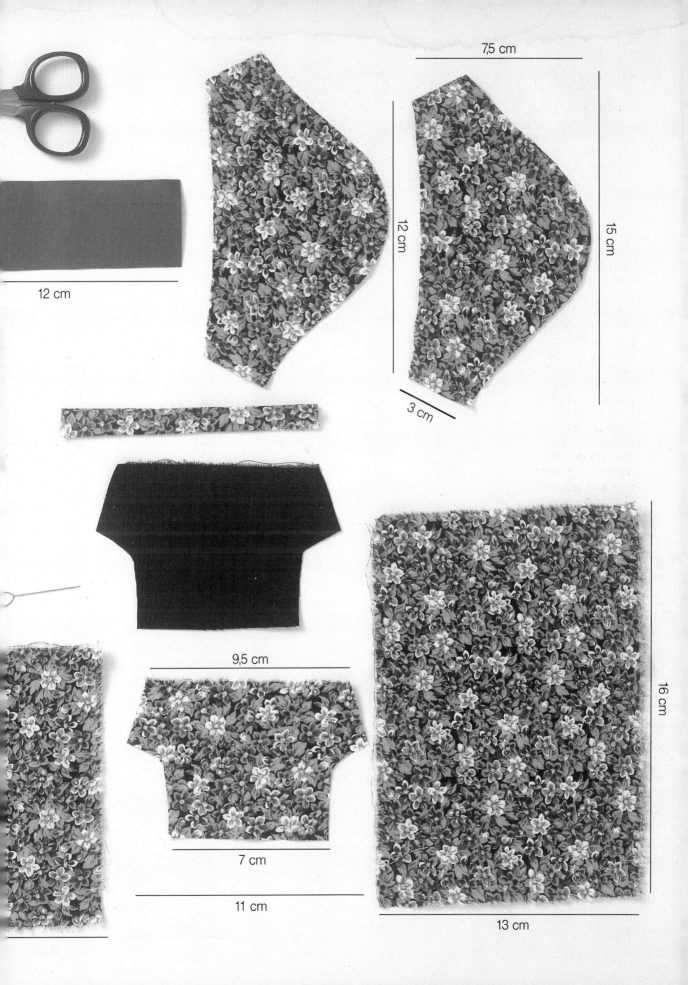

7,5 cm

12 cm

15 cm

12 cm

3 cm

9,5 cm

16 cm

7 cm

11 cm

13 cm

FOR THE LITTLE ONES

A baby girl is born and here is a lovely little trousseau ready for the new-arrival! Cap, socks, bibs, blouse, jumpers—all embroidered with strictly pink small roses to wish her a lovely day.

For the first outings in the pram, here is a lovely handmade cotton blanket embellished with a knit stitch embroidery. The small fawn sitting on the flowery meadow is looking at a butterfly with a certain curiosity. This is an amusing gift for a new mother or a little nephew or niece.

For the Baptism Ceremony, here is a family heirloom, a cap in handmade lace which gains even more importance if embroidered with small roses in silk ribbon on matching colored satin ribbons.

On the border in Aida cloth this beautiful crossstitch embroidery heralds the birth of a new child: a cascade of satin and organdie ribbons in different hues of light blue enriches the work.

INDEX